D0891484

Red Scare or Red Menace?

RED SCARE OR RED MENACE?

*American Communism and
Anticommunism in the Cold War Era*

John Earl Haynes

The American Ways Series

IVAN R. DEE   *Chicago*

RED SCARE OR RED MENACE? Copyright © 1996 by John Earl
Haynes. All rights reserved, including the right to reproduce this book or
portions thereof in any form. For information, address: Ivan R. Dee, Inc.,
1332 North Halsted Street, Chicago 60622. Manufactured in the United
States of America and printed on acid-free paper.

Library of Congress Cataloging-in-Publication Data:
Haynes, John Earl.
    Red scare or red menace? : American communism and
anticommunism in the cold war era / John Earl Haynes.
        p. cm. — (The American ways series)
    Includes bibliographical references and index.
    ISBN 1-56663-090-8 (cloth). — ISBN 1-56663-091-6 (paper)
        1. Communism—United States—History. 2. Anti-communist
movements—United States—History. I. Title. II. Series.
HX83.H36 1996
335.43'0973—dc20   95-40051

Contents

Preface

WHILE I WAS writing this book the Soviet Union collapsed, and in 1992 once-closed Soviet archives became open to Western historians. It was an opportunity I could not resist, and since 1992 much of my free time has been taken up with research visits to those archives and assimilating its previously unexamined historical documentation. While this opportunity delayed the completion of this manuscript, the time at the Moscow archives was well spent. The documents available in these archives, along with the release of hitherto secret U.S. government records also triggered by the end of the cold war, will significantly change how scholars treat the history of American communism and anticommunism. It will take some years before most historians comprehend how these new documentary sources alter what we know of historical events, and understand that the generally accepted premises underlying accounts of American communism and anticommunism over several decades are now obsolete.

In examining histories of American anticommunism in the late 1940s and 1950s, four deficiencies stand out. First, most accounts downplay or even deny the link between the American Communist party and Soviet espionage; second, they fail to delineate the historical continuity of post–World War II anticommunism with prewar antifascism; third, they fail to describe the breadth and variety of anti-Communist sentiment; and, fourth, they treat opposition to communism as irrational and inexplicable. To make American anticommunism in the 1940s and 1950s historically explicable is the purpose of this book.

I wish to thank Harvey Klehr and Ronald Radosh for sharing their observations on the *Amerasia* case, Lowell Dyson and

Herbert Romerstein for reading sections of the manuscript, and my publisher, Ivan Dee, and John Braeman, editor of this series, for their skilled editorial work in reducing the original manuscript to the length appropriate for this series as well as for their sorely tried patience with the delays necessitated by my work in Moscow's archives.

J. E. H.

Washington, D.C.
November 1995

Red Scare or Red Menace?

1

Communism and Anticommunism

COMMUNISM IS a movement embodied in a specific political party, the Communist Party of the United States of America (CPUSA) which articulates a specific ideology, Marxism-Leninism. The history of American communism is a history of that party and its splinters and of that ideology and its variations. Anticommunism, in contrast, has been a stance rather than a movement. There has been no anti-Communist party to lead a movement, nor has there been a core of anti-Communist ideology. Anti-Communists have been defined by what they are against rather than what they are for. Rather than a single anticommunism, there have been a multitude, with different objections to communism. The various anticommunisms did not follow a common agenda aside from their shared opposition to communism, or even necessarily approve of one another. What's more, at the height of public concern over anticommunism and the cold war, many groups and interests sought to use the issue as a tool to promote their individual agendas or as a weapon against those whom they opposed. All of this makes generalizing about anticommunism difficult. Anti-Communist activity has flowed from a variety of motives, has differed widely in its methods, and needs to be understood in the context in which it has occurred.

To understand anticommunism it is essential to keep in mind what communism was. A variety of ideologies derive from the teachings of Karl Marx, but only Soviet communism achieved and held power for any length of time, and it proved to be a catastrophe of epochal proportions. With German Nazism it has made the twentieth century a cruel age. Unlike Nazism, which explicitly placed war and violence at the core of its ideology, communism sprang from idealistic roots. Communists sought a revolutionary transformation of society into an egalitarian utopia of material and cultural abundance while freeing the human spirit from the constraints of ignorance, superstition, class oppression, race, ethnicity, and nationality. But Communists so hated the existing world that they willingly, even eagerly, used unlimited violence to bring about their envisioned just society. The coup that brought Lenin's Bolsheviks to power in Russia in 1917 and the subsequent Russian civil war were exceptionally vicious. In a typical order, Lenin in 1918 directed his subordinates in one rural area: "1) You need to hang (without fail so the *public sees*) *at least 100* notorious kulaks [property-owning farmers], the rich and the bloodsuckers. 2) Publish their names. 3) Take away *all* their grain. 4) Execute the hostages—in accordance with yesterday's telegram. . . . Yours, Lenin."

The climax of Communist mass murder occurred during the long reign of Joseph Stalin who gained control of the Soviet state after Lenin's death in 1924 and ruled until his own death in 1953. In 1929 Stalin initiated the collectivization of agriculture. When Soviet farmers resisted, Stalin responded with widespread executions and the deportation of millions to forced-labor camps or remote areas where many died of malnutrition and exposure. While scholars still argue about the total, somewhere between three and seven *million* men, women, and children died in the collectivization campaign.

In the mid-1930s Stalin launched an urban terror aimed at purging the Communist party and the Soviet state of all potential opposition to his total rule. Soviet secret police clandestinely executed more than a quarter-million persons and sent between five and ten million to forced-labor camps in Siberia (known as the Gulag) where a tenth or even a quarter died from malnutrition and overwork.

In 1939 the Soviet Union signed the Nazi-Soviet pact with Germany which allowed the Soviets to annex half of Poland, a sixth of Rumania, and all of Lithuania, Latvia, and Estonia, in return for pledged nonaggression against Hitler's forces. Between one-half and one million persons died during these annexations. After World War II the establishment of Communist regimes in Poland, East Germany, Bulgaria, Hungary, Rumania, and Czechoslovakia produced a new round of mass executions and deportations. Stalin ordered an expansion of forced-labor camps in the Gulag. By the end of the 1940s the number of political prisoners again reached into the millions.

In addition to mass terror, mass executions, and the system of forced-labor camps, Soviet communism created a totalitarian society in which virtually all aspects of social, economic, and cultural life were regulated by the Communist party. Freedom of the press, freedom of speech, and the rule of law did not exist. The Soviet criminal code punished a worker whose machine broke or a peasant whose field had excessive weeds for the economic crime of "wrecking." In 1930 Stalin, irritated by the delay of the Soviet central bank in remedying a coin shortage, ordered the government to "definitely shoot two or three dozen wreckers . . . including several dozen common cashiers." Similarly punished were thought crimes such as a joke about Communist authorities or an expression of disdain for the Bolshevik revolution or its achievements. This criminalization of any criticism of the state originated not with Stalin but earlier with Lenin himself. In 1922 he instructed those drafting the Soviet criminal code that "the law should not abolish terror; to promise that would be self-delusion or deception; it should be substantiated and legalized in principle, clearly, without evasion or embellishment."

Communists justified their rule by coercion as necessary to achieve social justice and material abundance. One American Communist leader confidently predicted that a society under Communist rule "would enjoy a wealth that would make the present affluence of the United States look like the contents of a brindle-stiff's [hobo's] bundle." But communism's promise of abundance failed. Before collectivization, Russia had been an exporter of grain and other agricultural goods. After collectivization, Soviet agriculture became so inefficient that it eventually turned to importing large quantities of food, and the quality of its food products was notoriously poor. Although the USSR enjoyed a bounty of natural resources, the industrial achievements of Soviet communism were second rate. In the 1980s the Soviet Union achieved the distinction of being the only "first world" nation with a falling life expectancy and a rising infant mortality rate. Beset by internal contradictions, the Soviet system fell into a crisis that by 1991 brought the disintegration of the Soviet Union and the end of Communist rule.

In 1934, while Stalin's collectivization program was killing Russian peasants by the millions, a much-praised American Communist poet, Tillie Olsen, described the Soviet Union as "a heaven . . . brought to earth in Russia." There is no doubt that many individual Communists thought they were creating a heaven on earth even while they were creating something much closer to a hell. The conflict between Communists and anti-Communists had an odd quality because communism combined within itself both soaring idealism and radical evil. Communism's opponents were often perplexed as to how they should deal with individual Communists who frequently exemplified communism's idealism—but who had worked assiduously to bring to power a system that wreaked enormous injury on its people.

Most Americans have never liked communism. Indeed, most have despised it. This dislike manifested itself with communism's birth in the Bolshevik revolution of November 1917. The Bolshevik triumph was a military disaster for America and its World War I allies, because Lenin withdrew Russia from the war and signed a treaty with Germany giving the kaiser victory in the East. Germany was thus able to shift hundreds of thousands of troops from the East to the Western Front and achieve superiority over the stretched French and British forces. With desperation the United States rushed hundreds of thousands of hastily trained soldiers to France. Many Americans blamed Lenin's Communist regime for the critical Allied position in early 1918 and for the deaths of American soldiers who fought and ultimately defeated the German troops who had been shifted from the Eastern to the Western Front.

The American Communist movement was formally founded in 1919. Revolutionaries inspired by Lenin's Bolsheviks left the more moderate Socialist party and founded two new parties: the Communist Party of America and the Communist Labor party. The two later merged. The newborn American Communists were forthright in their intentions, advocating the violent overthrow of the government and declaring, "Communism does not propose to 'capture' the bourgeois parliamentary state, but to conquer and destroy it." The Communist party platform clearly stated, "It is necessary that the proletariat organize its own state *for the coercion and suppression of the bourgeoisie.*" In addition to this frightening message, the newly organized American Communist movement was made up largely of immigrants, noncitizens and non-English speaking, reinforcing the image of communism as a foreign import. American Communists also drew overwhelmingly from political radicals who were already unpopular for having opposed the American war effort and called for avoidance of the military draft. During the war this had brought them heated patriotic attack and official prosecution.

Communist ideology was incompatible with the values held by most Americans. Americans have always held a variety of political views, but most support private property, take immense pride in their individualism, and glory in political democracy. Soviet communism, in contrast, abolished private property, instituted the collective, not the individual, as the basis of society, and established a one-party dictatorship that ruthlessly suppressed dissent. Most Americans are also religious and place considerable importance on their freedom to worship God as they please. The new Soviet state promoted atheism, suppressed Christian worship, and murdered thousands of priests and religious adherents. To many Americans, communism was a godless abomination.

Fear of bolshevism's spread was fed by the revolutionary movements that seized control of much of Central and Eastern Europe after the collapse of the German and Austro-Hungarian empires at the end of World War I. In the United States too there seemed to be signs of radical upheaval. In 1919 the police in Boston went on strike, an inherently frightening development, and Seattle experienced a brief general strike led by an admirer of the Bolsheviks. More than half a million steel workers also struck; their leader, an avowed radical named William Z. Foster, later became a leading Communist. Radical terrorists launched a bombing campaign that killed thirty-five and injured more than one hundred persons before it ended. Bombs exploded simultaneously in eight cities in June 1919, and a number of individuals were targeted with letter bombs. The targets included Attorney General A. Mitchell Palmer, members of President Wilson's cabinet, the mayors of Seattle and Cleveland, John D. Rockefeller, J. P. Morgan, and other business leaders, legislators, judges, and churches. The deadliest bomb exploded September 16, 1920, at lunch hour in the Wall Street district of New York City. With the world in ferment, Charles Ruthenberg, the first leader of the American Communist movement, confidently predicted that "new Soviet governments will arise as the months go by and it will not be long until the . . . Soviet Republic of the World comes into being."

Federal and local authorities responded with a wide-ranging crackdown on radical activity in the United States. In late 1919 and early 1920, Attorney General Palmer launched a series of raids aimed at alien radicals, arresting more than five thousand persons. U.S. authorities retained those who were noncitizens for deportation. U.S. citizens picked up in the "Palmer raids" were turned over to state and local police for prosecution under state antisubversive laws.

New York City was home to many newly born American Communists. In the fall of 1919 New York police raided dozens of radical clubhouses, arrested several hundred persons, and confiscated large quantities of radical literature. The raids produced plenty of proof of revolutionary agitation but almost no evidence of bomb-making or terrorist activity. Most of those arrested were later released, but seventy-five were tried under various New York laws. Two of the Communist movement's chief founders,

Charles Ruthenberg and Benjamin Gitlow, received sentences of five to ten years each but actually served less than three.

The heated atmosphere of the "Red Scare," as it was later called, provoked both federal and local agencies to disregard normal legal restraints on official power. During the raids officials often failed to obtain search or arrest warrants from judicial authorities, and those arrested were in many cases abused and held incommunicado. Initially few citizens complained of the excesses of the Palmer raids, but later a number of prominent citizens denounced their abuses. The U.S. Labor Department, which had jurisdiction over immigrant matters, also blocked Palmer's plans to deport alien radicals without a hearing and simply on presentation of evidence of revolutionary activity. Consequently the majority of those arrested in the Palmer raids were released. Several hundred immigrants were deported before the hearing requirement was imposed, and about six hundred were deported after hearings established their revolutionary loyalties.

By 1921 the Red Scare was over. Fears of world revolution faded. Striking Boston police were fired and replaced, the Seattle strike collapsed, and the steel strike failed. The bombers were never tried, but police collected enough evidence to identify the likely perpetrators and place them under surveillance; the bombings ceased. In Europe anti-Communists overthrew short-lived Red regimes in Bavaria, Hungary, Latvia, and Finland. A Bolshevik invasion of Poland failed in 1920, and German authorities smashed a Communist uprising in 1921. Lenin's government survived in Russia and even conquered the briefly independent nations of Ukraine, Georgia, and Azerbaijan, but it was otherwise isolated and exhausted. President Warren G. Harding, who took office in 1921, spoke for many when he observed that "too much has been said about Bolshevism in America." Public interest diminished, and widespread legal attacks on the Communist movement waned though occasional local harassment continued.

Over the next decade the American Communist party went through complex internal changes but remained a small

movement without influence whose members were chiefly immigrants who spoke little English. Indeed, without the massive
secret financial subsidies that American Communists received
from the Soviet Union, the movement might have collapsed altogether. Throughout most of its existence, the American Communist party employed an extraordinary number of full-time
employees, several hundred in the 1920s expanding to several
thousand in the 1930s and 1940s, when its control of a number of
union locals allowed it to place additional cadre on union payrolls. While the party eventually developed a bank of wealthy
American benefactors, generous Soviet subsidies were often critical to its ability to employ so many professional revolutionaries.
After the Soviet Union collapsed, documents in Moscow archives
confirmed these secret subsidies. As late as 1988 a KGB agent delivered to Gus Hall, general secretary of the CPUSA, $3 million in
cash.

In addition to large financial subsidies, the Soviet Union
brought hundreds of Americans to the USSR for political and
organizational training at special Communist schools and sent
veteran Communist revolutionaries to the United States to ad-
vise the American movement. The Communist International
(known as the Comintern), a Soviet-controlled organization that
supervised non-Soviet Communist parties, established a special
"American Commission" that reviewed the activities of American Communists. American Communist leaders traveled to
Moscow to make lengthy reports to the Comintern and received
detailed instructions for American Communists. The Comintern
also settled factional fights within the American party and sub-
stituted its own choices for leadership positions. After communism collapsed in the Soviet Union, American historians were
astounded to find in newly opened Soviet archives many thousands of pages of documents dealing with the American Communist party and showing minute Moscow supervision of the
American movement.

But communism and anticommunism were peripheral issues
to most Americans during the 1920s. After the end of the Red
Scare most of the organizations that had worried about commu-

nism turned to other issues. The Justice Department eliminated most of the internal security apparatus it had created during World War I. Army and Navy military intelligence officers, active during the war in surveillance and prosecution of antiwar radicals, continued from time to time to check on Communist activities, but the military in the interwar period was small and lacked jurisdiction over civilian activity. The professional officer corps regarded its peacetime intelligence service as a dumping ground for incompetents and mavericks. Military intelligence officers more than once wrote alarmist reports of Communist activity and found their reports filed away by an indifferent military bureaucracy. The many private patriotic organizations that had exposed or harassed antiwar radicals also disappeared. Those that remained were small, mere letterhead organizations kept going by a few enthusiasts (or fanatics) seeking to keep alive the righteous patriotism of wartime. Although there remained a broad and deep public dislike of communism, it could be aroused only when events suggested that communism was a real threat rather than the ravings of street-corner radicals or the ideology of a distant, weak, and isolated Soviet Russia.

The Great Depression proved to be a promising environment for the Communist Party U.S.A., or CPUSA as it was titled in 1929. The nation's economic disarray damaged faith in market economics and undermined confidence in capitalism and traditional institutions; to some Americans the depression seemed proof of the validity of Communist ideology. Communists also adopted a stance more appealing to those Americans who were looking for a political answer to the disaster of the depression. This policy had its origins in Moscow.

Until the early 1930s fascism had not been perceived by the Soviet Union as a major threat. Germany's powerful Communist party, at Moscow's urging, refused to assist either the centrist parties or the left Social Democrats against Hitler's Nazis. Communists reasoned that Hitler's rise to power would bring on a crisis in Germany, after which they would be able to create a Red state. Hitler, however, consolidated his power and crushed not only the centrists and moderate-left Social Democrats but German Communists as well. Hitler's expansionist goals and rearmament program prompted Stalin to conclude that the USSR itself was at risk. The growing strength of fascism in other European nations, particularly France, raised fears that without coalitions with other political forces, Communists elsewhere would suffer the same grim fate as they had in Germany.

Thus in 1935 Moscow formally called for a "Popular Front" against fascism that could include moderate political parties. In response, American Communists put aside their revolutionary rhetoric and sought common ground with liberals by supporting President Franklin Roosevelt's New Deal reforms at home and a foreign policy that opposed fascist aggression abroad. The changes paid off and the CPUSA began to grow, gaining a majority of native-born members in the mid-1930s and reaching a membership of 65,000 to 70,000 members in 1939.

In the mid-1930s Communists also dissolved their small collection of revolutionary labor unions and sent their members into the mainstream labor movement of the American Federation of Labor (AFL). When, frustrated with the slowness of the AFL to organize workers in mass-production industries, the Congress of Industrial Organizations (CIO) broke away from the AFL, the new CIO leaders needed experienced and dedicated organizers quickly, and so decided to use Communists. John L. Lewis, head of the infant CIO, secretly negotiated with the Communist party to provide hundreds of its professional trade union organizers to the CIO. This opportunity allowed Communists to become the dominant partners in the leadership of one large CIO union, the United Electrical Workers, and more than a dozen smaller CIO affiliates. CPUSA officials supervised the activity of CIO Communists, received detailed reports from Communists in leadership positions, provided financial assistance for Communist activists, and organized secret caucuses of Communist union militants to agree on tactics before important union meetings.

Communists presented themselves as the left wing of the broad New Deal coalition and in a few states and cities entered mainstream politics. Some liberals accepted the Popular Front as a permanent change in Communist philosophy and reached out to Communists as allies against conservatism and big business. The *New Republic* and *The Nation*, leading journals of American liberalism, adopted a Popular Front stance and championed an alliance between liberals and Communists. In New York, Communists became a force within the American Labor Party, a CIO-aligned state-level party that held the balance of power between the Republicans and Democrats. In Wisconsin, Communists became part of the left wing of the La Follette–led Progressive party that dominated state politics in the mid-1930s. In Minnesota, Communists became a powerful force in the Farmer-Labor party that controlled state government in the mid-1930s. In Washington, Oregon, and California, Communists won a measure of influence in the liberal wing of the Democratic party. Two members of Congress were secret members of the CPUSA: Representatives John Bernard (Farmer-Labor party, Minnesota) and Hugh DeLacy (Democrat, Washington). A significant Communist presence in local Democratic party politics could also be found in Detroit and Chicago.

Communists ceased being pariahs and gained a measure of respect and even of admiration from influential intellectuals and artists. In 1932 the CPUSA's presidential ticket was endorsed by such leading American writers as Sherwood Anderson, Theodore Dreiser, Lincoln Steffens, and John Dos Passos. Several of the nation's most productive playwrights and film writers, including Clifford Odets, John Howard Lawson, and Donald Ogden Stewart, became Communists. Communists sponsored and secretly controlled the League of American Writers and the American Artists' Congress, bodies that brought together leading figures from literature and the arts behind a Popular Front program.

The improved position of American communism was directly linked to a more favorable view of the Soviet Union. The view developed that Stalin's rise to the leadership of the USSR actually signaled a moderating of the Bolshevik revolution. Thus the *Chicago Tribune*, a leading voice of hard-right conservatism, gleefully interpreted Stalin's execution of rival Bolshevik leaders as the "liquidation of the Red Revolution." And many American liberals came to believe that New Deal America and Stalin's Russia were on a converging path. Sumner Welles, confidant of President Roosevelt, said that FDR believed that "if one took the figure 100 as representing the difference between American democracy and Soviet Communism in 1917, with the United States at 100 and the Soviet Union at 0, American democracy might eventually reach the figure 60 and the Soviet system might reach the figure of 40."

At the same time the Communist party was gaining respectability, it was also establishing an underground organization headed until 1938 by J. Peters (or Jozip Peter), a senior party official. The existence of the CPUSA underground was long a matter of dispute among historians, but documents found in Soviet archives after the fall of Soviet communism show that it was a fact. One report from the head of Soviet military intelligence spoke of "one of the Communist groups that the leadership of the American Comparty has chosen for informational work is operating in Washington. That group is headed by . . . 'Peter.' " With documents about the underground were stolen copies of U.S. State Department correspondence. This underground carried out a number of missions, including seeking out ideological deviation within the party and guarding against infiltration of the party while infiltrating organizations hostile to the movement. Another task, supervised by Peters himself, was the placement of concealed Communists in selected government agencies in order to gain information or to influence policy. This tactic too is confirmed by documents found in Russia. The chief government agencies in which secret Communist caucuses operated in the 1930s included the Agricultural Adjustment Administration (1934 and 1935, largely dispersed by 1936), and the Civil Liberties Subcommittee of the Senate Labor and Education Committee (1935–1939), the National Labor Relations Board, the National Youth Administration, the National Research Project of the Works Progress Administration, and the Treasury

Department. As one document found in the Soviet archives stated, referring to the infiltration of a single government agency, ". . . There are Communists taking part in the work of that commission (Roosevelt is unaware of this). Communists found their way into that commission through the Communist faction of Washington officials."

While much of the CPUSA's infiltration of government agencies was of limited importance, the secret Communist presence constituted a serious abuse in several cases. In the National Labor Relations Board, for example, the hidden Communist caucus biased its activities to help those labor unions that had Communist leadership. By 1940 this problem had become sufficiently troublesome to the Roosevelt administration that it brought in new officials, reshuffled the NLRB's staff and forced out Nathan Witt, the board's secretary (executive director) and a secret Communist, and thereby largely broke up the Communist group inside the National Labor Relations Board.

Although the CPUSA's underground apparatus in the U.S. government was chiefly involved in promoting the party's political goals, it also cooperated with and provided recruits for Soviet intelligence agencies engaged in espionage against the United States. Those cases came to light after World War II and played a major role in arousing popular anticommunism.

The 1930s was the heyday of American communism, but there were limits to American acceptance. Most public opinion surveys found very large majorities of Americans disapproving of communism. In most areas of the nation, politicians regarded open association with Communists as a liability, and Communists who worked in mainstream politics as part of a Popular Front alliance normally concealed their Communist loyalties from all but their closest allies. Even in the CIO, where Communists were a powerful minority among union activists, worker hostility to communism was such that almost every CIO Communist concealed his Communist allegiance. Still, anticommunism had only limited saliency as a national political issue in the 1930s. Roosevelt, for example, had little difficulty in brushing off

Republican attempts to portray his administration as too tolerant of Communists. Although most Americans were viscerally anti-Communist, as long as Communists kept a low profile and presented themselves as "progressives," most Americans were not inclined to push the issue.

2

Fascism and World War II

WHEN AMERICANS of the 1930s looked for a threat to their way of life, it was not communism but Adolf Hitler's goose-stepping legions that seemed more menacing. The American response to Nazism and fascism in the 1930s established important precedents for post–World War II anti-Communist activities.

Nazism was quickly recognized by most Americans as a radically evil movement, and it had few American admirers. Unlike communism, Nazism had its origins not in idealism but in the raising of national chauvinism and anti-Semitic hatred into an all-encompassing ideology. Nazis glorified violence and militarism and hid only the most monstrous of their acts, unlike Communists who habitually hid their brutality behind a curtain of idealistic propaganda.

In addition to the brutal nature of the Nazi regime's internal rule, Hitler unsettled Americans by overturning the World War I peace settlement. With astounding defiance, he began a massive rearmament program, occupied Germany's Saar and Rhineland border regions (demilitarized under the accord ending World War I), and annexed all of Austria and most of Czechoslovakia.

Hitler's success also encouraged fascist movements in other European nations. French fascists came close to overthrowing France's weak Third Republic. Both Hitler and Italy's fascist dictator, Benito Mussolini, sent troops and supplies to assist General Francisco Franco in his attack on the Spanish Republic in the

Spanish Civil War of 1936–1939. Franco's forces won and established a dictatorship with strong fascist elements. Fascism, not communism, appeared on the march in the 1930s.

In the American mind one feature that made fascism in the 1930s seem particularly threatening was its appearance of having created a new strategy of combining internal political subversion with external military aggression. During the Spanish Civil War, Franco's army advanced on Madrid, the besieged capital of the Spanish Republicans, in four columns. The general directing the offensive boasted that he had a secret "fifth column" of fascists inside the city sowing disaffection and defeatism, one that would assail the Republicans from within as his troops assaulted the city's defenses from without. Thus was born the image of the fifth column as a clandestine underground that spread political subversion, engaged in sabotage, and prepared the way for military conquest.

Fifth-column imagery grew stronger as Hitler used covertly organized Nazi sympathizers, first in Austria and then in Czechoslovakia, to pave the way for German annexation. A classic success of the fifth column was the surprise German assault on Norway in 1940. Secret Nazi sympathizers led by Vidkun Quisling sabotaged the mobilization of the Norwegian armed forces and, once German forces occupied the nation, installed themselves as leaders of a Norwegian government allied with Nazi Germany. ("Quisling" thereafter became a pejorative term for a traitor and fifth columnist.)

French fascists and right-wing extremists disenchanted with the weak French Third Republic also spread defeatism and fear of another hideous bloodletting like World War I. When Hitler's blitzkrieg hit France in the summer of 1940, French morale cracked and the government collapsed, replaced by the "Vichy" regime of French fascists and far-right conservatives hostile to liberal democracy.

In the United States, William Donovan, a famous World War I military figure and a well-known Republican, and Edgar Mowrer, an influential journalist, published *Fifth Column Lessons for America*. Using the French experience, they warned Americans that "a situation like that of France might arise" because "none can estimate the number of Hitler's allies, conscious or unconscious, in this country." This highly exaggerated view that the fifth column was a serious menace to the United States received government endorsement at the highest level. President Roosevelt in a radio address to the nation attributed Hitler's success to "the Trojan Horse, the fifth column that betrays a nation unprepared for treachery. Spies, saboteurs and traitors are the actors in this new tragedy."

Much of the popular image of American communism that appeared after 1945 was based on attitudes developed in the 1930s and early 1940s toward fascism. In particular, the image of the American Communist party as a fifth column for the Soviet Union drew directly on late 1930s images of Nazi fifth-column activity. And the techniques developed to fight American fascism and American fifth-column activity in the 1930s were the same as those used against American Communists in the late 1940s and 1950s.

In retrospect, the American fascist menace was more an image and a possibility than a reality. The German-American Bund, the best-known pro-Nazi organization in the United States, was made up almost entirely of recent German immigrants. While fanatically pro-Nazi, the Bund never functioned as a fifth column. German intelligence did use the Bund as a recruiting ground for spies; several Bundists carried out espionage missions for Germany, and one Bund leader returned to Germany to train Nazi saboteurs who were later sent to the United States during World War II. (All were captured and most were executed.) But the Bund had no significant political influence, little money, and its cooperation with profascist groups of native-born Americans was limited. Its newspaper seldom reached a circulation of more than ten thousand, and Bund membership at its peak was less than that. The Bund's chief political activity was holding rallies where its members showed off their uniforms (modeled on those of the Nazi party's storm troopers) and made violent, hate-filled speeches denouncing Jews and praising Hitler's Germany. Most of the Bund's rallies were small; more than once, anti-Nazi protesters outnumbered the Bundists.

The largest American fascist organization was William Dudley Pelley's Silver Shirts. Pelley, who openly proclaimed his desire to be America's dictator, promoted a strange creed that mixed fascism, anti-Semitism, and religious doctrines that included reincarnation. His Silver Shirts organization reached a peak membership of about fifteen thousand in 1934 but lost two-thirds of that by 1938. The most brutal quasi-fascist organization was the mysterious Black Legion operating in the industrial Midwest. Not much is known of its ideology beyond its raging hatred of immigrants, Jews, blacks, and Catholics. The Legion's membership was small, probably only a few hundred men in a secret brotherhood. It engaged in several violent assaults on persons it disliked, murdered several people, but fell apart when thirteen of its members were tried for murder and the ringleaders jailed for life. In 1936 two Hollywood films were based on this obscure group: *Black Legion* (a dramatic success featuring Humphrey Bogart) and *Legion of Terror*. For dramatic effect, both films exaggerated the Black Legion as a widespread menace with secret cells throughout America.

Gerald Winrod, a fundamentalist Protestant preacher headquartered in Kansas, organized the Defenders of the Christian Faith and sought to establish an American fundamentalist Christian republic free of alien and corrupt modern influences. Winrod came to identify Roosevelt's New Deal as the Jewish- and Communist-controlled Antichrist of the biblical Book of Revelation. Although not a fascist (he glorified neither violence nor militarism and did not call for the overthrow of America's constitutional order), Winrod was intensely anti-Semitic and admired Hitler. He had a following in Kansas, and his newspaper reached a peak national circulation of 110,000 in 1938.

In the mid-1930s the Roman Catholic priest Charles Coughlin gained a large national radio audience with his message combining communitarian Catholic social doctrines with a populist economic program attacking big business and big banks. For a time his radio audience numbered in the millions, but his popularity declined rapidly in the late 1930s as Coughlin became increasingly anti-Jewish and extremist. Coughlin also became allied with the small Christian Front in New York. Christian Fronters, largely impoverished Irish and German Catholics, blamed the nation's problems on Jewish bankers and engaged in military training (a picture of President Roosevelt was often used as the target in rifle practice). Christian Front gangs on several occasions beat Jews who ventured into New York's Irish neighborhoods.

Despite their extremism and potential for violence, none of these groups constituted a fifth column or a serious fascist menace. The Silver Shirts, like the Bundists, occasionally found themselves a minority at their own rallies. Although rumors abounded of big business providing various fascists with millions of dollars, neither the Silver Shirts, the Bund, nor any of the extremist organizations displayed signs of financial prosperity. On the contrary, they appeared to live in a continuous state of financial crisis. The German-American Bund never received from Nazi Germany anything approaching the subsidies the American Communist party received from the Soviet Union. The various extremists did not cooperate and often disliked each other. The anti-Catholic Black Legion or the fundamentalist followers of Gerald Winrod, for example, could scarcely have cooperated with Father Coughlin or the largely Catholic Christian Front.

Nor did the extremists have much influence on elected officeholders. Coughlin could never translate his huge radio audience into a coherent voting bloc. In 1936 he backed the Union party and the presidential candidacy of William Lemke, a maverick Republican congressman from North Dakota. The Union party was a political failure; Lemke won only 891,858 votes compared with 27,243,466 for President Roosevelt and 16,681,913 for Alfred Landon, the Republican candidate. Gerald Winrod made one serious try at elected office, but even in Kansas, the center of his strength, the best he could do was a poor third in a Republican Senate primary. A few malcontent members of Congress occasionally cooperated with one or another extremist organization.

In 1931 Representative Louis T. McFadden, a veteran Pennsylvania Republican, began cooperating with Pelley and his Silver Shirts; he promptly lost his seat in 1932, and all his later attempts to regain public office failed. In 1938 Montana elected Jacob Thorkelson to the U.S. House of Representatives. Thorkelson, a Republican, turned out to be a strident anti-Semite, and he publicly associated himself with William Pelley and the Silver Shirts. He too lost his seat in the next election, and his later tries for public office were defeated. Association with fascists in the 1930s was as damaging to an elected politician as association with Communists would be after World War II.

The failure of the Bund, Pelley and his Silver Shirts, and other profascist groups to constitute either a fifth column or a significant political force was not due to a lack of inclination on their part. There never was a serious American fascist menace in part because American fascism was exposed, denounced, and defeated before it could find a sustaining constituency.

A large antifascist literature of exposure discredited the various pro-Nazi and fascist organizations. The most successful was John Carlson's *Under Cover: My Four Years in the Nazi Underworld* (1943). Carlson's account of his infiltration of various quasi-fascist organizations sold a million copies. Major newspapers serialized the book, and a film version also appeared. Carlson's reports of what he had done and seen were largely accurate, and the organizations he described were as evil as he said, but his melodramatic rhetoric painted an exaggerated picture of a vast and highly menacing Nazi fifth column preparing to disrupt the United States. Carlson's writings also reflected his political view that opposition to President Roosevelt's foreign policy was tantamount to sympathy for Nazism.

Other works by active antifascists, such as *I Find Treason: The Story of an American Anti-Nazi Agent* by Richard Rollins, told much the same story. A 1940 book, *The Fifth Column Is Here*, claimed that there were a million fifth columnists in the United States prepared to rise against the government. Gaetano Salvemini in *Italian Fascist Activities* and Robert Strausz-Hupe in *Axis America* put the number of Italian-Americans loyal to Mussolini's fascism at a ridiculously high 200,000. The popular magazine *Saturday Evening Post* ran stories with such titles as "Hitler's Weapon Against Us," describing America as facing a serious Nazi fifth-column menace. *Life* magazine, *Christian Century*, and the *New York Times* chimed in with similar stories. Boy's adventure books, such as the popular Dave Dawson series, also carried to America's youth the message of the fifth-column danger. All this agitation about the fascist-Nazi menace had its effect. For a period in 1940, after the Nazi conquest of Western Europe, citizen reports to the FBI of possible fifth-column activities exceeded two thousand a day.

Motion pictures, one of the most popular entertainment mediums of the era, championed the anti-fascist message. *Confessions of a Nazi Spy*, a 1939 Warner Brothers film, depicted the German-American Bund as a spy organization that sought America's military mobilization plans, blueprints for U.S. battleships, troop locations, and information on the Panama Canal, all as part of a Nazi plan to invade the United States. The 1940 film *Arizona Gang Busters* worked the fifth column into the popular cowboy film genre by having U.S. Marshal Tiger Tim Rand smash a plot by fifth columnists to take over an Arizona ranch for a base of operation. Similarly, in the 1941 film *King of the Texas Rangers* the heroic Rangers uncover a fifth-column plot to sabotage Texas oil fields. In 1943 Roy Rogers in *King of the Cowboys* exposed a Nazi fifth column (headed by a fifth-columnist state governor) intent on blowing up a railroad bridge when a troop train crossed it. Another popular 1943 film, *Air Force*, blamed the successful Japanese attack on Pearl Harbor on sabotage of American defenses by a well-organized fifth column.

Many government officials were convinced of the seriousness of the domestic Nazi menace. Roosevelt took a personal interest in right-wing extremism and in 1936 ordered the Federal Bureau of Investigation, which had largely withdrawn from the internal security field in the mid-1920s, to reenter the area. FBI director J. Edgar Hoover welcomed Roosevelt's orders to revive the Bureau's antisubversive program and endorsed the idea of the existence of a powerful Nazi/fascist underground. Hoover's

FBI and the Justice Department also leaked information on the Bund and domestic fascists to journalists in order to expose their activity.

The German-American Bund became the major target of American antifascists. The American Legion and the Veterans of Foreign Wars (VFW) demanded that the Bund be outlawed and its leaders deported. The Legion and VFW also hired private investigators to infiltrate the Bund's camps to gather evidence that could be used to outlaw the organization. In several incidents, protesters organized by local American Legion clubs violently disrupted Bund meetings. Often municipal authorities refused to rent the Bund public arenas (other far-right extremists had the same problem on occasion), and the organization also had trouble finding private owners willing to rent a meeting hall for a rally. During the antifascist era, right-wing extremists found limits to free speech, just as during the anti-Communist era there were limits to freedom of speech for Communists.

Congressional committees repeatedly investigated Pelley's Silver Shirts, the German-American Bund, and several other extremist right-wing groups. In 1940 Congress enacted a law forbidding the employment of Bundists by the federal government, and denied unemployed Bundists relief work from the depression-era Works Progress Administration. That same year two Bund activists who had become U.S. citizens had their naturalized citizenship revoked, one for selling Nazi literature which a naturalization examiner found to be incompatible with American citizenship. New York and New Jersey also outlawed the Bund's wearing of storm trooper–like uniforms.

The most serious official blow to the Bund before American entry into World War II was delivered by New York authorities. In 1939 New York City Mayor Fiorello La Guardia ordered city tax officials to seize the Bund's financial records. Ostensibly the revenue agents were checking on the Bund's tax status, but in fact they were on a fishing expedition for any prosecutable crimes. The records showed that Fritz Kuhn, head of the Bund, had converted $14,548 in Bund funds to his personal use, including support for a mistress. The Bund, which operated according to the Nazi *Führerprinzip* that its leader had absolute control, endorsed Kuhn's authority to spend Bund money as he wished. With most organizations, a refusal to complain of embezzlement probably would have foreclosed prosecution, but New York District Attorney Thomas E. Dewey saw a chance to cripple the Bund and brought criminal charges. Kuhn was convicted. His imprisonment badly disrupted the Bund's leadership, and it never recovered.

Although the American Legion and other veterans' organizations were prominent (and sometimes violent) in the antifascist campaign, liberal and left groups were the most ardent antifascists. The Friends of Democracy, organized in 1939 by prominent liberals such as the philosopher John Dewey and the writer Thomas Mann, specialized in what it called "pitiless publicity." Its goal was exposure of Nazi, fascist, and right-wing extremists. The Friends of Democracy prepared dossiers on eight hundred "pro-Nazi and Fascist" organizations. The dossiers, based on press clippings, informant reports, copies of speeches, and organizational literature, were made available to friendly journalists for the preparation of stories exposing the Nazi/fascist menace.

Even harsher in its antifascism was the American Council Against Nazi Propaganda and its journal, *The Hour*. The leading figure in the Council was William E. Dodd. Roosevelt had appointed Dodd, a prominent liberal historian, as U.S. ambassador to Germany in 1933. He had gained much stature among Americans during his ambassadorship by his public disapproval of Nazism. Dodd was convinced that Hitler had many supporters in the United States, and on his return to America in 1938 declared, "Fascism is on the march today in America. Millionaires are marching to the tune. It will come in this country unless a strong defense is set up by all liberal and progressive forces." American Communists were also major although secret backers of the American Council Against Nazi Propaganda. Much of the Council's research staff and many of the writers for *The Hour* were concealed Communists.

According to the American Council Against Nazi Propaganda there were "548 Hitler-groups in 45 foreign countries manned by 25,000 propaganda agents and 2,450 special Gestapo hirelings." This "Nazi espionage-and-propaganda machine" was directed "toward its aim: a Nazi America." *The Hour* published an index listing the names and addresses of hundreds of far-right extremists, calling the list "a bird's-eye view of the U.S. fifth column, a catalogue of American Quislings and their machinations." The Council also urged the government to investigate professors that *The Hour* suspected of fascist sympathies—at Yale University, the University of Minnesota, Columbia University, Brooklyn College, Hunter College, and Stanford University.

The Hour exposed the marital troubles of the leader of the quasi-fascist Crusaders for Americanism and forced the firing of two other leading profascist agitators by exposing them, listing their employers, and urging its readers to complain to the companies that employed them. The journal also exposed Lambert Fairchild, the host of an NBC radio program, as having links to quasi-fascist organizations in early years and charged that anyone who associated with his program was thereby tarred with the same brush. Specifically it accused the well-known dramatist Maxwell Anderson of having written a radio play for Fairchild's program. *The Hour* quickly received a letter from Anderson in which he pleaded ignorance of Fairchild's background and apologized for his actions. Anderson's play had been a dramatization of religious persecution under Nazism, but neither the antifascist theme of the play nor Fairchild's carrying it on his program was sufficient to restrain *The Hour*'s attack on Fairchild for his past links to domestic far-right extremists. The journal renewed its attacks by exposing Fairchild's marital and bad debt difficulties in the 1920s. With satisfaction, *The Hour* reported that the organization that sponsored Fairchild's program had fired him in response to *The Hour*'s campaign.

The strident antifascism of the American Council Against Nazi Propaganda and *The Hour* was echoed by many liberals in the 1930s. In *The Nation* in 1933 a prominent leftist blamed the spread of fascism in Europe on excessive civil liberties and urged the United States not to make the same mistake. Lewis Mumford, a prominent liberal intellectual, called for a ban on fascist literature from the mails and exile or imprisonment for fascist leaders. The University of Miami removed literature regarded as pro-Nazi or profascist from its library. Several states passed group libel or hate-speech laws making it a crime to print or speak in a derogatory fashion about any ethnic group, measures usually aimed at anti-Semitic speech. Virtually every one of the tactics used in the 1930s and early 1940s to harass fascist and suspected far rightists would after World War II be used against Communists and those suspected of left-wing sympathies.

In another precedent for postwar anticommunism, antifascism also proved too powerful a weapon not to be used for partisan political purposes. George Earle, the New Deal Democratic governor of Pennsylvania, proclaimed without a scrap of evidence that "the money changers and the great industrialists behind the Republican party leadership" were behind the quasi-fascist Black Legion. A 1937 book, *The Fascist: His State and His Mind*, claimed that two pillars of the business community, the National Association of Manufacturers and the Chambers of Commerce, were financing an American Nazi uprising. When Louisiana's Huey Long began to attack President Roosevelt, the liberal journalist Raymond Gram Swing asserted that Long had plans to become the Hitler of America. Although the American Legion was one of the Bund's chief opponents, Swing denounced it along with the Fraternal Order of Elks for their "pattern of fascist action." The liberal writer George Seldes asserted that the American Legion was really part of the "Fascist International" and that the *Reader's Digest* was covertly fascist.

Some antifascists also faked evidence when it served their needs. The *March of Time*, a popular news documentary shown weekly in many movie theaters, frequently ran segments warning of the domestic fascist threat. One of its targets was Gerald L. K. Smith, a vile anti-Semitic demagogue, but not a fascist. When the *March of Time* ran a segment on Smith with crowds of supporters giving him the fascist salute, Smith sued. He received only one dollar for damages, but he won a backhanded admission that the film of the crowd giving him the fascist salute was faked.

After the outbreak of the war in Europe in September 1939, American debate over the nation's policy toward the war and the threat of domestic fascism intensified and became the subject of partisan exploitation. Although most Americans disliked Hitler and sympathized with Britain and France in their struggle against Nazi Germany, opinion about the U.S. course of action was much more divided. President Roosevelt favored generous American aid to the anti-Nazi belligerents and, as Nazi conquests expanded, sought to bring American power onto the scales against Hitler. Opposing Roosevelt's policies was a large body of public opinion and a significant portion of the Congress that, while hostile to Hitler, was adamant in opposition to U.S. intervention in the war.

The leading voice against Roosevelt's foreign policy was the America First Committee, which included persons of all stripes who opposed intervention, including many pacifists, but was predominantly led by conservative Republicans. The America First Committee's leadership realized that association with Nazism would taint their cause and in the main succeeded in keeping the organization free of infiltration by anti-Semites and pro-Nazis who wished to use its large following as cover for their own agenda.

President Roosevelt and his supporters, however, strove to tar America First with the Nazi brush. Roosevelt charged that the leaders of the America First Committee were "unwitting aides of the agents of Nazism." The Friends of Democracy flatly called America First a "Nazi front" and suggested that Charles Lindbergh, the famous airman and America First's most prominent spokesman, was a secret Nazi. Arguing that America First was a potential fifth column, the Friends of Democracy urged the government to institute FBI surveillance of America First's members.

While the FBI did not undertake such a surveillance, with President Roosevelt's authorization it began to tap the telephones and open the mail of vocal opponents of his foreign policy and monitor anti-intervention rallies. As part of this program the

FBI also instituted surveillance of several of the president's prominent congressional critics, including Senators Burton Wheeler (Democrat, Montana) and Gerald Nye (Republican, North Dakota). The White House and the Justice Department also leaked to antifascist journalists information from FBI files that was embarrassing to anti-interventionists. The Democratic and liberal campaign was largely successful, and those who opposed intervention in World War II became tagged with the politically opprobrious term "isolationist." These isolationists and right-wing Republicans who were unfairly tainted were greatly angered by the excesses of the campaign against them. When the political atmosphere changed after World War II, their bitterness would produce a strong drive for revenge using similar tactics against their liberal and Democratic opponents.

After Germany declared war on the United States in December 1941, U.S. authorities used wartime security measures to destroy what was left of the German-American Bund. Officials seized the Bund's assets and arrested several dozen of its leading members. In 1943 Fritz Kuhn and ten other Bundists were stripped of their naturalized citizenship on the ground that Bund membership was incompatible with U.S. citizenship. Kuhn was deported to Germany in 1945. The war also gave President Roosevelt his long-sought opportunity to prosecute would-be *Führer* William Pelley of the Silver Shirts. By this time Pelley's magazine had a subscription list of only about 3,500 and his speeches seldom drew a crowd unless it was a hostile one. Even so, the Justice Department, with one of Roosevelt's aides supervising, prosecuted Pelley on the ground that his publications were damaging the war effort. The principal tactic used in the prosecution was to point out similarities between Pelley's statements and those of Nazi and Japanese propagandists. Pelley received a fifteen-year sentence; two of his subordinates received five years in prison. The government also banned Father Coughlin's journal *Social Justice* from the mails. With the encouragement of the government, Coughlin's superiors in the Catholic church ordered him to cease all public activity, an order he obeyed. He dropped from public sight and his following, now only a fragment of what it had been before he turned extremist, disappeared.

Government investigators never uncovered a real fifth column. The FBI turned up evidence that Nazi intelligence recruited Bund members for espionage, and Wilhelm Kunze, Kuhn's successor as head of the Bund, went to prison for his cooperation with German spies. Authorities also found evidence that German and Japanese agents helped several dozen right-wing extremists, usually anti-Semites, to finance their publications. A few cases of Japanese funding of extremist black nationalists also turned up. Altogether, several hundred Bundists, Silver Shirts, other American fascists, and anti-Semitic extremists were imprisoned for publishing or giving speeches judged to interfere with military recruiting, or for accepting financial subsidies from foreign agents. The government also seized a fraternal insurance company with forty thousand members (mostly Ukrainian immigrants) and $6 million in assets when it determined that some of the insurance company's officials had links to profascist bodies.

In 1941 the government used the Smith Act to imprison eighteen leaders of the Socialist Workers party (Trotskyists) who advocated revolutionary resistance to American war mobilization. (Trotskyists were dissident Communists who adhered to the views of Leon Trotsky, a Soviet leader who was first exiled and then murdered by Stalin.) In a precedent that would later have considerable irony, American Communists cheered on the government's prosecution. In order to assist the government charge that the Trotskyists were revolutionaries, CPUSA leaders even provided prosecutors with Socialist Workers party speeches and publications that Communists had collected regarding their hated ideological rivals.

The government also indicted twenty-eight American fascists and right-wing extremists for violation of the Smith Act and the Espionage Act. Those indicted were a motley crew, including a few well-known names such as Pelley (already in prison on other charges), Gerald Winrod (The Kansas fundamentalist anti-Semite), and Elizabeth Dilling (a vocal advocate of the view that

Roosevelt's New Deal was a Jewish-Communist conspiracy). Some of those tried in this case were more nutty than dangerous, such as two leaders of the National Workers League, an anti-Semitic organization, who also turned out to be the *only* members of the National Workers League.

Initially the government charged that the defendants' speeches and writings in and of themselves constituted a criminal conspiracy to incite insubordination in the armed forces. Prosecutors cited advocating the impeachment of President Roosevelt, blaming his policies for getting the United States into the war, blaming Roosevelt for racial miscegenation, and comments supporting the foreign policies of Germany, Italy, and Japan. Proving that this variegated group was part of a single criminal conspiracy was not easy, however. The case dragged on into 1943, and the government reformulated its charges and in the process dropped simple advocacy as a crime. Instead it emphasized conspiracy to encourage insubordination in the armed forces and taking money from foreign nations while failing to register as foreign agents. In November 1944 the death of the judge trying the case produced a mistrial. The case by this point had become an embarrassment to the government, and prosecution was dropped in 1946.

Although American Communists had been among the most militant antifascists, after the August 1939 treaty between Hitler and Stalin they dropped out of the antifascist movement and became the target of antifascist anger. The Nazi-Soviet pact came as a surprise to American Communists, but they dutifully and swiftly shifted their political stance in response to a series of messages from Moscow instructing them on their new policy. In mid-September 1939 the CPUSA announced that the conflict between Nazi Germany and the Western Allies was an imperialist war, that both Nazi Germany and those who fought Hitler were "equally guilty," and demanded that the United States remain neutral. A CPUSA journal explained, "The previous alignment into democratic and fascist camps loses its former meaning. The democratic camp today consists, first of all, of those who fight against the imperialist war." The *People's World*, the West Coast Communist paper, called Britain "the greatest danger to Europe and all mankind" and denounced Winston Churchill, Britain's leader, as a "raving maniac." And Communists bitterly denounced Lend-Lease aid to Britain as a "Blue-Print for American Fascism."

The Communists' abrupt about-face after the Nazi-Soviet pact had serious consequences for the party's hard-won status within American society. Most of the front groups that had achieved prominence were destroyed or severely weakened by defections of liberals unable to stomach the new policies. The League of American Writers, a Popular Front body to which many well-known authors belonged, lost most of its prominent members. The Communist-aligned National Lawyers Guild similarly lost many of its liberal members. A. Philip Randolph, an influential black union leader, broke with the National Negro Congress when, at the insistence of its concealed Communist leaders, it denounced Roosevelt and praised Soviet policy after the Nazi-Soviet pact.

The anti-Roosevelt stance of CIO Communists was so at variance with the sentiments of most union members that it gave CIO anti-Communists their first wedge to crack the Communist position in the CIO. In Minnesota, for example, a Communist-led Popular Front faction had long controlled the state CIO council. Communists used their influence in 1940 to get the Minnesota CIO to denounce Roosevelt as one of the "enemies of the People" and to urge workers to cast blank ballots in the presidential election. Anti-Communists in the Minnesota CIO had been in disarray, but using support for Roosevelt as a rallying point, sprang forward as an organized caucus with more than a third of the votes at the state CIO convention. Communists and their allies in the Minnesota CIO beat back the attack but were forced to drop the incumbent head of the Minnesota CIO, whose Communist membership was well known. They replaced him with a new leader whose CPUSA membership was a better-kept secret.

The Communist position in the CIO would have been worse had it not been that John L. Lewis, the CIO's leading figure, was an anti-interventionist and hostile to FDR's foreign policy. As long as Lewis headed the CIO, the Communists could use his prestige and his anti-Roosevelt position to protect themselves from the backlash against their attack on Roosevelt. But in 1940 Lewis backed Republican Wendell Willkie for president and stated that if workers failed to heed his stand, he would relinquish the leadership of the CIO. When union workers voted heavily for Roosevelt, Lewis turned the leadership of the CIO over to Philip Murray. Once Lewis resigned, anti-Communist caucuses in a score of CIO unions and central bodies went on the attack, forcing CIO Communists onto the defensive.

CIO Communists' support of strikes in war industry plants also roused the ire of the Roosevelt administration. When Communist union officials supported the shutdown of a vital California aircraft factory, an enraged President Roosevelt privately accused Communists of using their union positions to sabotage arms production. On Roosevelt's orders, the army seized the plant and broke the strike. Roosevelt's indignation at Communist tactics, along with his fear of the development of a fifth column, resulted in a decided shift in government policy. In 1939 Roosevelt signed the Hatch Act, which included a section denying federal jobs to members of organizations advocating the overthrow of the government. In 1940 he signed the Smith Act, which required all noncitizens to be fingerprinted and register their addresses with the federal government, made it a crime to interfere with the loyalty or discipline of the armed services, and included a sedition statute aimed at both fascists and Communists. In 1941 Roosevelt authorized his secretaries of War and Navy to dismiss summarily any government employee under their jurisdiction deemed a concern to national security.

The Roosevelt administration also hit directly at the leadership of the Communist party by imprisoning Earl Browder, the CPUSA's general secretary, for his use of forged American passports for travel to the Soviet Union. U.S. authorities discovered Browder's passport fraud years earlier but sat on the information until the Nazi-Soviet pact. In 1940 Roosevelt also signed the Voorhis Act, requiring foreign-controlled organizations to register with the government and provide information on their activities, a statute aimed both at the German-American Bund, several Italian-subsidized profascist organizations, and the Communist party. The CPUSA was officially the U.S. section of the Communist International, headquartered in Moscow. (For a time American Communist membership cards read "The undersigned declares his adherence to the program and statutes of the Communist International. . . .") Rather than comply with the Voorhis Act, the CPUSA officially ended its affiliation with the Communist International. As a practical matter, this made little difference. As archives revealed after the collapse of the Soviet Union, CPUSA leaders continued to report to the Comintern and take its orders on the same basis as before.

During the Popular Front era of the 1930s many commentators accepted the Communist and fascist self-definitions that they were polar opposites of each other. The first dissenters from this view were liberal and left-wing anti-Communist intellectuals. The latter argued that even though Communists and fascists hated each other, the two movements were sibling rivals. In this analysis the two movements held so many common features that they could be seen as opposite wings of a single twentieth-century phenomenon: totalitarianism. The hallmark of totalitarianism was a society wherein all private and public institutions (economic, social, cultural, political, governmental, educational, and intellectual) became permeated with and mobilized by the ruling party-state. Those taking this view developed the expression that Soviet communism was really "Red fascism" and Nazism was "Brown bolshevism."

The Red fascism analysis was a decidedly minority view among politically conscious intellectuals in the 1930s—until the Nazi-Soviet pact. But when fascism became to Communists, in the words of Soviet Foreign Minister V. M. Molotov, "a matter of taste," this assessment received a new hearing. The Hitler-Stalin alliance and all that flowed from it provided such startling confirmation that Nazism and communism had much in common that for a time Red fascism became the reigning view among political commentators.

Because of the large reservoir of anti-Communist sentiment in the American population, the public easily accepted the Red fascism analysis and assimilated Communists into their fears about an American Nazi/Fascist fifth column. Red fascism was so quickly accepted that it found its way into a 1940 movie, *Death Rides the Range*. This film featured the FBI hunting down Soviet agents who were in league with American fascists attempting to steal helium (then regarded as strategically important) from gas wells in the American West. Similarly, state governments that had moved against Bundists and other fascists in the late 1930s also moved against Communists after the Nazi-Soviet pact. Thirteen states prosecuted Communists during this period, jailing between three hundred and four hundred for short sentences. It is unlikely that these prosecutions would have been undertaken had not Communist activities during the Nazi-Soviet pact made them both disliked and feared due to pervasive fifth-column anxiety.

By mid-1941 American communism was increasingly vulnerable. Then, on June 22, 1941, Hitler threw over his alliance with Stalin and invaded the Soviet Union. American Communists immediately shifted from fervent opposition to American involvement in World War II to impassioned support for U.S. intervention. After the United States entered the war and became a military ally of the Soviet Union, the CPUSA unreservedly threw its support behind the American war effort and behind Roosevelt's war policies.

The Nazi-Soviet pact had lasted only a year and a half, and the CPUSA's enthusiasm for the war effort afterward repaired much of the damage done to relations with liberals. Government prosecution ceased, and as a gesture of goodwill toward the Soviet Union, just before a visit to Washington by Molotov, President Roosevelt commuted Earl Browder's sentence to time served and released him. Still, the Nazi-Soviet pact had done irreparable damage to American Communists. Some New Deal liberals attuned to the Popular Front atmosphere of the 1930s had received a rude demonstration that no Communist principle was as important as loyalty to the Soviet Union. Communists reestablished the Popular Front after June 1941, but a very large measure of trust and goodwill had been lost. Communists would pay dearly for this loss when the cold war shattered the Popular Front once more.

By the end of the war, Communists regained most of the support they had lost during the Nazi-Soviet period. In the first two years following World War II, American communism achieved its greatest institutional power. The CPUSA's membership reached about 70,000, roughly matching its peak in 1939, with a large majority being native-born Americans. International Publishers and New Century Publishers, both party aligned, published more than a million books and pamphlets each year. Circulation of the *Daily Worker*'s Sunday edition often exceeded 50,000 while weekday issues of the party newspaper exceeded 20,000. In addition, the party maintained more than a dozen foreign-language newspapers that circulated in the tens of thousands in various immigrant communities. The CPUSA also controlled the International Workers Order, a fraternal insurance company whose membership reached about 185,000. But the CPUSA's greatest source of institutional power was its role in the CIO, where unions with Communist-aligned leaders represented about 1,370,000 unionists, a quarter of the CIO's total. Their power within the labor movement gave Communists entrée into mainstream politics. All these achievements, however, became vulnerable once the cold war began.

3

The Road to the Cold War

WORLD WAR II ENDED with most Americans confident that U.S. power was unchallengeable. In 1945 the U.S. navy and air force were without peer, and the U.S. army, while not the world's most powerful (the Soviet Red army held that distinction), was both formidable and easily the best equipped in the world. Further, with the atomic bomb the United States had a monopoly on the ultimate weapon. Most Americans felt that between the strength of America's economy, the power of its military, the safety of its ocean barriers, and its monopoly of the atomic bomb, no one could threaten the nation.

What followed, however, was not the peace that most Americans expected. The wartime alliance of the Soviet Union with the United States and Great Britain rapidly disintegrated. American expectations that the Soviet Union would retire to its prewar or at least to its 1941 boundaries proved illusory. While Britain and the United States rapidly demobilized their armed forces, Stalin maintained a huge contingent of the Red army in Eastern Europe and installed Communist governments throughout the region. The Soviets erected a border of barbed wire, mine fields, watch towers, and armed guards to keep the people of Eastern Europe from fleeing Communist control. Britain's Winston Churchill captured Western dismay (and coined one of the common phrases of the cold war) in a 1946 speech in Fulton, Missouri, in which he observed, "From Stettin in the Baltic to Trieste in the Adriatic, an iron curtain has descended across the conti-

nent." In the Far East, civil war broke out in 1946 in China between the nationalist government of Chiang Kai-shek and Chinese Communists under Mao Tse-tung. By 1949 all of mainland
China, the world's most populous nation, fell to the Communists,
and Chiang's forces retreated to the island of Taiwan. Soviet
troops also installed a Communist regime in North Korea, and
armed Communist insurgencies made serious bids for power in
Vietnam, Burma, and Malaysia. Communism was on the march.

The Western response was initially uncertain but steadied in
late 1946 and 1947 when President Truman launched the United
States into the cold war. Since 1945 the Soviets had been de-
manding that Turkey cede part of its territory to the Soviet
Union as well as grant the USSR military bases and rights to
partial control of the strategic straits between the Black Sea and
the Mediterranean. This Soviet diplomatic campaign became
more threatening in mid-1946 and hinted of military action. In
response Truman ordered U.S. naval forces to the eastern
Mediterranean and quietly urged the Turks to resist. The immediate crisis passed when the USSR, in the face of the American
military moves, withdrew its threats against Turkey.

The crisis in the eastern Mediterranean was renewed in early
1947 when the British government informed Truman that
Britain's severe economic difficulties required withdrawal of
British military aid to Turkey and Greece. Civil war had broken
out in Greece in 1945 between Communists and anti-Communists,
and only British military intervention had prevented a Communist takeover. No American military aid supported either nation,
and British withdrawal was expected to lead to Communist victory in the Greek civil war as well as renewed Soviet pressure on
Turkey.

Truman responded by asking Congress to authorize U.S. military aid to Turkey and Greece. In so doing he called for a national commitment, known as the Truman Doctrine, that it be
"the policy of the United States to support free peoples who are
resisting attempted subjugation by armed minorities or by outside pressure." "At the present moment in world history," Truman told Congress, "nearly every nation must choose between

alternative ways of life.... One way of life is based upon the will of the majority.... The second way of life is based upon the will of a minority forcibly imposed upon the majority." A second part of Truman's cold war strategy appeared in June 1947 when Secretary of State George Marshall announced a plan for massive American economic aid to deal with a severe European economic crisis that was threatening to bring powerful Communist parties to power in Italy and France.

The Truman Doctrine and the Marshall Plan were about more than the immediate problems in Greece and Turkey or Europe's economic crisis; they were a declaration of hostilities in the cold war and committed the United States to the containment of Communist expansion around the globe. Congressional support for these cold war policies rested in large part on the rapid mobilization of anti-Communist sentiment. The groundwork for this mobilization was prepared during World War II, even while the Soviet Union was America's ally.

In August 1941, in the midst of the war in Europe, President Roosevelt and British Prime Minister Churchill had pledged their nations to "respect the right of all peoples to choose the form of government under which they will live; and they wish to see sovereign rights and self-government restored to those who have been forcibly deprived of them." The agreement, called the Atlantic Charter, stated the "desire to see no territorial changes that do not accord with the freely expressed wishes of the peoples concerned." Roosevelt mingled the principles of the charter with his earlier enunciation of the "Four Freedoms," in which he said America looked forward at the end of the war to "a world founded upon four essential human freedoms: The first is freedom of speech and expression—everywhere in the world. The second is freedom of every person to worship God in his own way—everywhere in the world. The third is freedom from want— ... everywhere in the world. The fourth is freedom from fear— ... anywhere in the world."

After the United States entered the war, Roosevelt formally proclaimed the Four Freedoms and the Atlantic Charter to be

America's war aims. All of America's wartime allies, including the Soviet Union, also pledged their support to the Atlantic Charter. The Office of War Information, the government's chief propaganda agency, made the Four Freedoms and the Atlantic Charter central themes of its massive public relations campaign. Millions of placards, pamphlets, radio broadcasts, newspaper ads, movie newsreels, and motivational lecturers bombarded the public and the newly created mass armed forces with the promises of the Four Freedoms and the Atlantic Charter.

During the war 400,000 American military personnel died and nearly 700,000 suffered wounds, but victory was won. Yet the democratic postwar world which was to justify the bloodletting was fulfilled only in part. Western Europe was liberated, but the Four Freedoms and the Atlantic Charter were not realized in Eastern Europe. The annexation of Lithuania, Estonia, and Latvia, half of Poland, and parts of Rumania and Finland by the USSR, and the Soviet Union's imposing subservient tyrannies upon Poland, Hungary, Czechoslovakia, Rumania, East Germany, and Bulgaria surprised and shocked a great many Americans. The shock expressed itself in the rapid revival of popular anticommunism.

Young liberal veterans were among the most politically important groups angered by the failure of Roosevelt's democratic promises. They had reached their adulthood during the war and had imbibed the heady idealism of wartime liberalism and the wartime Popular Front. The most politically active of these liberal veterans founded a new veterans' organization, the American Veterans Committee, as an alternative to the conservative American Legion and the Veterans of Foreign Wars. In its initial stands after World War II, the American Veterans Committee took a distinctly Popular Front line, supporting American cooperation with the Soviet Union in order to build the peaceful democratic postwar world promised by the wartime Popular Front. This posture changed as news came out of Eastern Europe that Communist rule was being forcibly imposed and that tyranny, not democracy, was to be the postwar order in those areas under Soviet domination. Inside the American Veterans Committee, caucuses formed along lines that would later be replicated in the larger liberal community. A Popular Front–aligned caucus organized around the defense of the Soviet Union's hegemony in Eastern Europe and urged American accommodation to this in the interests of peace. In opposition was an anti-Communist caucus which angrily denounced Soviet actions as the cynical breaking of wartime pledges and treaties that had promised the peoples of Eastern Europe freedom to decide their own destinies. Leaders of the anti-Communist caucus inside the American Veterans Committee included many figures who would later play major roles as liberal anti-Communists. They included G. Mennen Williams, later governor of Michigan; Franklin D. Roosevelt, Jr., the president's son and later a New York congressman; Gaylord Nelson, later governor of and U.S. senator from Wisconsin; Henry Reuss, later a longtime Wisconsin congressman; Orville Freeman, later governor of Minnesota and U.S. secretary of agriculture; Donald Fraser, later a Minnesota congressman; Gus Tyler, an aide to David Dubinsky of the International Ladies' Garment Workers Union and later a major figure in liberal politics; and Gilbert Harrison, publisher of the influential *New Republic*.

After four years of struggle the anti-Communist caucus prevailed, but the American Veterans Committee as an organization was by that time a lost cause. The bitter factional battle had discouraged most rank-and-file veterans from joining. The Committee remained small and was never able to create a powerful liberal veterans' organization.

One of the largest mass constituencies jolted toward an anti-Communist stance by the disjuncture between Roosevelt's democratic war aims and postwar events were the many millions of first- and second-generation ethnic Americans of Eastern European origin. Of these groups, the largest were Polish Americans; the 1940 census showed nearly three million Americans were of first- or second-generation Polish origin, and the third generation would have added further to this total. Polish Americans were not only a large community, they were also highly sensitive to Polish national issues because of the severe wartime travail of the Polish nation. World War II began on September 1, 1939, when Nazi armies crashed into Poland. The Polish cause became hopeless on September 17 when, with most Polish forces engaged by the Nazis in the west, the Red Army invaded Poland from the east. By early October all of Poland was occupied, and in accordance with the Nazi-Soviet pact Germany and the USSR divided Poland in two. Under Nazi rule five million Poles (about three million Polish Jews and two million Christian Poles) either were murdered or died of deprivation. While Hitler killed Poles in the millions, Stalin killed them in the hundreds of thousands. Most notable was the secret execution of approximately fifteen thousand captured Polish army officers in the Katyn forest near Smolensk and at several other sites. The USSR annexed eastern Poland and deported a million to a million and a half Poles living in this area to remote regions of the USSR; several hundred thousand died of deprivation.

After fleeing Poland, the Polish government reached London and continued to fight, supporting an anti-Nazi underground "Home Army" in occupied Poland and recruiting an exile army of 300,000 men from among Poles who were living abroad or who had escaped during the fall of Poland. The Polish government-in-exile and Polish Americans knew that any hope for a favorable outcome for Poland after Hitler's defeat rested with the United States holding the Soviet Union to its promises to support the principles of the Atlantic Charter.

In May 1944 anxious Polish ethnic leaders formed the Polish American Congress, an umbrella organization of twenty thousand Polish fraternal lodges, parishes, cultural associations, sports and youth groups, veterans' posts, newspapers, and fraternal insurance companies. The Congress dedicated itself to winning American support for a free and independent Poland within its prewar boundaries, which included the half of Poland that Stalin had annexed. The call for the founding convention stated that "the Congress will declare the wholehearted cooperation of support of Americans of Polish descent of the declarations of our President pertaining to the Four Freedoms and the At-

lantic Charter, that nations, large or small, might exist by themselves free of all interference and aggression."

Polish-American voters were among the New Deal's most
loyal constituencies, with many Polish districts habitually turning in 70 percent or better Democratic majorities. Any disquiet
that might reduce these majorities was a major political problem.
During the 1944 presidential campaign, Roosevelt held two
highly publicized meetings with the Polish American Congress,
one in the White House and one in Chicago. The president
promised the anxious Poles that the Atlantic Charter would be
upheld and, though refusing formally to commit himself on the
question of Poland's borders, he held his Washington meeting in
front of a huge wall map of Poland showing its prewar boundaries. Based on these meetings, Charles Rozmarek, head of the
Polish American Congress, endorsed Roosevelt for reelection. In
the 1944 election Polish precincts turned in their usual overwhelming Democratic majorities.

While these assurances served Roosevelt's and the Democratic
party's short-term political purpose, they were not fulfilled. In
the long term they contributed to an angry upsurge in anti-
Communist sentiment. In part the promises were sincerely
meant, but FDR assumed, mistakenly, that Stalin's ambitions
were modest. Even George Kennan, the State Department's
leading Soviet specialist, wrote in 1944 of Soviet ambitions in
Eastern Europe, "It is a matter of indifference to Moscow
whether a given area is 'communistic' or not."

In addition to this erroneous view of Stalin's policies, a measure of evasion also occurred. Although Roosevelt told Polish-
American leaders that he had made no concession to Stalin on
Poland at the Teheran Conference of Allied leaders, in fact he
had. Roosevelt agreed to the Soviet annexation of eastern Poland
(with German land given in partial compensation) but explained
that the deal must not be formally announced because, as he told
Stalin and Churchill, "there were in the United States from six to
seven million Americans of Polish extraction, and as a practical
man, he did not wish to lose their vote." During 1944 Roosevelt

met with Prime Minister Stanislaw Mikolajczyk of the Polish exile government. Roosevelt urged Mikolajczyk to drop anti-Soviet members from his cabinet and assured him that the Soviets did not intend to interfere with Poland's internal governance if Polish foreign policy accommodated Soviet security needs. On the margins of a memorandum describing Mikolajczyk's meeting with Roosevelt, Anthony Eden, then Britain's foreign secretary, wrote, "The President will do nothing for the Poles, nothing more than [U.S. Secretary of State] Cordell Hull did in Moscow or the President did himself in Teheran. The poor Poles, it is sad that they delude themselves if they believe in those vague and lavish promises. Later, the President will not keep them at all."

In 1944 Stalin set up the Polish Committee of National Liberation run by Communists, with nominal non-Communist figureheads, as an alternative to the government-in-exile. Although the United States officially recognized the government-in-exile, Averell Harriman, the U.S. ambassador in Moscow, met with the Committee of National Liberation, thus signaling American willingness to treat it as a legitimate force.

American officials began to realize they had badly misjudged the Soviets in August 1944. By then the Red Army had driven the Nazis back into Poland and was within twenty miles of Warsaw. The underground Home Army decided to free Warsaw of Nazi control before the Red Army arrived, in order to make the liberation of their capital city a Polish achievement. They also hoped their seizure of Warsaw would strengthen their position in the struggle to control liberated Poland. In the first three days of fighting the Home Army's 25,000-man Warsaw contingent took control of large parts of the city.

Once the revolt began, however, the Red Army's offensive stopped; around Warsaw the Soviets barely moved for months. Hitler, meanwhile, ordered his forces to besiege Warsaw and put down the Home Army revolt with savage ferocity. In the face of anguished cries from the Poles and then from British and American diplomats, the Soviets replied that their forces were temporarily unable to move due to supply problems. Nor would

Stalin allow British and American aircraft to use Soviet airfields to drop munitions and supplies to the embattled Home Army until it was too late to make a difference. Home Army forces held the city for more than a month but surrendered to the Nazis in October after the death of about 15,000 Home Army soldiers and more than 75,000 Polish civilians. By allowing the Nazis to destroy the Home Army's Warsaw contingent, Stalin removed a powerful opponent of Communist domination of postwar Poland. After the Red Army resumed its offensive, NKVD security police units following the Red Army finished the job by disbanding Home Army units and arresting its officers.

Shaken by the Soviet response to the Warsaw uprising, Ambassador Harriman in 1945 told the State Department, "The time has come for us to reorient our whole attitude and our methods of dealing with the Soviet government.... Unless we wish to accept the 20th Century barbarian invasion of Europe ... we must find ways to arrest the Soviet domineering policy."

For Poland it was too late. The United States might have influenced events in Eastern Europe in 1942 and 1943, when the Soviet Union's military situation was precarious, American supplies were vital to the USSR's war effort, and the Soviets needed American and British military cooperation in order to relieve Nazi pressure on the Eastern Front. Perhaps then the United States could have won concessions from Stalin. But in those early days Roosevelt feared Soviet military collapse or another Nazi-Soviet pact in which the two dictators made a second division of Eastern Europe. In any case, Washington made no attempt to pressure Stalin and by late 1944 no longer had the leverage to force concessions from the Soviets even if it had tried—and it never tried.

Further, Roosevelt still wanted the Soviets for the Pacific war. While the United States and the United Kingdom were at war with both Germany and Japan, the Soviet Union was at war only with Germany. After the defeat of Germany, FDR wanted Stalin to invade Manchuria, draw off Japanese forces from the defense of the home islands, and perhaps convince the Japanese to surrender without the butchery of an invasion. The cost of pressing the Soviets too far on Poland might be reckoned in hundreds of thousands of Americans killed in the invasion of Japan. While such a cold-eyed realism may justify his policy, Roosevelt never explained this to the American people and particularly not to Polish Americans nor to other Eastern European ethnics worried about Soviet intentions. Instead Roosevelt and other Democratic leaders repeatedly assured them that the promises of the Atlantic Charter and the Four Freedoms would be fulfilled.

In late 1944 and 1945 there was nothing left for the American government but to play out a weak hand on Poland. In January 1945 the Soviet Union ignored the Polish government-in-exile and recognized the Polish National Liberation Committee as the provisional government of Poland. In February 1945 at the Yalta Conference of the Allied leaders, the only concessions Stalin would make were vague promises to include members of the government-in-exile in the Communist-dominated provisional government and to hold free elections. Even then, Roosevelt did not prepare Americans for what was to come. Instead he told the American people that the Yalta Conference assured a peace "based on the sound and just principles of the Atlantic Charter" and called the accord "the most hopeful agreement possible for a free, independent, and prosperous Polish state." Privately William Leahy, the president's chief of staff, told Roosevelt that Stalin's promise was "so elastic that the Russians can stretch it all the way from Yalta to Washington without even technically breaking it." Roosevelt replied, "I know, Bill—I know it. But it's the best I can do for Poland at this time." When Molotov, the Soviet foreign minister, complained to Stalin about Roosevelt's pressing the Soviet Union to reaffirm its pledge to allow those freed from Nazi rule to choose their new governments, Stalin replied, "Don't worry. . . . We can deal with it in our own way later."

Stalin allowed the provisional government to take in a few adherents of the government-in-exile, including Stanislaw Mikolajczyk, but it remained firmly under Communist control. The United States abandoned the exile government. Because they

were regarded as hostile by Poland's new Communist government, most of the soldiers of the Polish government-in-exile
became refugees. In Poland the provisional Communist government set about establishing a totalitarian party-state modeled on
Stalin's USSR. More than fifty thousand Poles were imprisoned
as potential political opponents of the new regime, and thousands died when Home Army units resisted Communist demands to surrender their officers and weapons. Stalin had
promised Roosevelt free elections in Poland. In January 1947,
after a campaign of terror, intimidation, and blatant fraud, the
provisional government announced that the people of Poland
had voted overwhelmingly for Communist rule. Stanislaw
Mikolajczyk fled into exile. Poland remained a tyranny for another forty years until the regime was overthrown by the Solidarity labor movement.

As the tragedy of Communist Poland unfolded, Polish Americans were appalled. Many believed that Poland's fate was the result of Soviet perfidy along with mistakes, though well
intentioned, by the Roosevelt administration. Others, however,
thought the administration had cynically misled them during the
1944 election campaign. A bitter Representative John Lesinski
(Democrat, Michigan), who had appealed to Polish Americans to
support Roosevelt in 1944, announced that at Yalta the president
had betrayed the Atlantic Charter for which American soldiers
had died. Charles Rozmarek, head of the Polish American Congress, had endorsed Roosevelt in the 1944 presidential campaign:
in 1948 and 1952 he pointedly endorsed the Republican presidential nominees. Also endorsing the Republican candidates in 1948
and 1952 was the former ambassador to Poland, Arthur Bliss
Lane. Lane had served as American ambassador after World
War II and had observed firsthand the methods used to establish
Communist rule. Deeply embittered by his experience, Lane resigned in 1947 as a protest against the bankruptcy of America's
Polish policy.

In the years after Yalta, in any district with a substantial Polish vote, congressional candidates had to be clearly anti-Soviet
and anti-Communist or face almost certain defeat. Several previ-

ously safely Democratic congressional districts with large Polish-
American constituencies swung to the Republicans when the
local Democrats did not shift to an anti-Communist stance
swiftly enough. In 1950, for example, Republican Timothy
Sheehan, campaigning on the betrayal of Poland at Yalta and
promising to investigate the Katyn massacre, won election in a
heavily Polish and usually Democratic Chicago congressional
district.

Polish-American voters numbered in the millions, and millions of other East European ethnic voters held grievances
against the Soviets similar to those of the Poles. Their defection
from the New Deal coalition would have been a crippling blow
to the Democratic party. Democrats responded to the anti-Soviet
anger among Polish Americans by embracing it and making it
their own. The Truman administration admitted large numbers
of anti-Communist Polish refugees and embraced Mikolajczyk
and others driven into exile in 1945–1947. The Democratic National Committee hired Michael Cieplinski, a naturalized Pole,
to direct its nationalities division with special emphasis on Polish
Americans. In 1948 President Truman, like FDR before him,
met with Polish-American leaders at the White House in front
of a huge map of Poland with its prewar boundaries. At Truman's direction, the 1948 Democratic platform also included a
specific endorsement of a Poland independent of Soviet domination.

In direct response to Timothy Sheehan's use of the Katyn issue
to win election in a normally Democratic Polish district, congressional Democrats hurried to take the leadership of the issue away
from Republicans. In 1951, with the endorsement of Democratic
leaders, Representative Ray Madden, an Indiana Democrat with
a Polish-American constituency, introduced a resolution calling
for congressional investigation of the Katyn massacre. It passed
by a vote of 398 to 0. President Truman supported the House's
Katyn hearings and instructed executive agencies to assist the investigation. This largely succeeded in turning Polish-American
rage about Katyn away from the Democrats and Roosevelt. Even
so, the hearings produced evidence to reinforce the belief that

some American officials had acted with duplicity by covering up evidence about the massacre. In its official report the House Katyn Committee concluded that during the war the U.S. government had collected evidence of Soviet guilt for Katyn but had "brushed aside" the information for fear that the truth would "hinder the prosecution of the war to a successful conclusion." Two Republican members of the committee issued a harsher judgment that saw the Roosevelt administration's treatment of Katyn as "a small part of the giant error made in our foreign policy program."

The revelations of the Katyn investigation about U.S. government participation in covering up Soviet guilt encouraged suspicion of sinister forces at work. The investigation also fed Polish-American mistrust created by the failed promises of the Atlantic Charter and the Four Freedoms and the sense of having been manipulated in the 1944 election. In 1946 Charles Rozmarek of the Polish American Congress told those gathered in Chicago to celebrate Polish Constitution Day, that he supported a "move to purge all Communists and those of the same mind as Communists from our government payrolls." Rozmarek called for a "thorough investigation of all the subversive activities of all 'Russia firsters' who are out to ruin our democratic form of government." In 1947 the Polish American Congress sponsored the formation of the Committee to Stop World Communism, chaired by former ambassador Arthur Bliss Lane. Lane's anger over what had been done to Poland would take him into the camp of one of the most strident and irresponsible anti-Communists, Senator Joseph McCarthy.

Despite the turn to the Republicans by Ambassador Lane and others upset over Poland, the Democratic party succeeded in retaining the loyalty of millions of Polish-American and other Eastern European ethnic voters. It did so by embracing anticommunism, sloughing off its Popular Front wing, and, through President Truman, establishing itself as the initiator of America's cold war policies. The arousal of anti-Communist sentiment among Polish Americans, and a similar mobilization of anticommunism among other immigrant groups, was not solely or even chiefly responsible for the Democratic party's shift, but it was a significant contributing factor.

As cold war tensions sharpened, revelations of Soviet espionage linked to American Communists renewed the image of the American Communist movement as a treasonous fifth-column peril. In February 1945, while reading the latest issue of *Amerasia*, a magazine devoted to problems of Asian politics and foreign policy issues, an analyst of the Office of Strategic Services (OSS), America's chief World War II intelligence agency, was jolted to find buried in one of the articles, several lengthy paragraphs lifted from a secret OSS report he had written on Thailand. While the stolen paragraphs in the *Amerasia* essay were not especially revealing, the report they had been taken from was highly sensitive because it also discussed in detail the leaders of the resistance movement then waging a guerrilla campaign against Japanese forces occupying Thailand. If the OSS report fell into the hands of the Japanese they would be able to decapitate the Thai resistance. Alarmed OSS security officers moved at once, breaking into *Amerasia*'s offices at night to see if they could determine how the magazine had got hold of an OSS classified document.

Inside *Amerasia*'s office OSS security men found evidence of much more than an isolated leak. They found photocopies of more than four hundred classified documents (several thousand pages), some classified as Top Secret, including documents on the strategic bombardment of Japan, recent intelligence reports on Japanese naval movements, and sensitive U.S. reports about intimate matters involving Chiang Kai-shek, the leader of the Chinese government. Markings on the documents showed that while the papers had originated from a variety of U.S. agencies, most bore stamps indicating that they had been received by the State and Navy departments.

The OSS turned over its findings to Secretary of State Edward Stettinius and Secretary of Navy James Forrestal, who then called in the FBI. FBI agents surreptitiously entered the offices of *Amerasia* and the residences of its employees, and FBI surveillance turned up more classified documents and established that three government employees were supplying the journal with information. The FBI arrested Emmanuel Larsen, a mid-level State Department official, as the chief source and seized more than two hundred classified documents from his private residence. It also arrested Lieutenant Andrew Roth, a navy intelligence officer; John Service, an up-and-coming foreign service officer; Philip Jaffe, editor and publisher of *Amerasia* (another six hundred classified documents were seized in Jaffe's office); Mark Gayn, a well-known journalist (classified documents were also found in his residence); and Kate Mitchell, another *Amerasia* editor.

What followed was a security scandal with an ambiguous outcome that would typify many of the espionage cases of the post–World War II era. The arrests closed a security breach, but the speed of the action had its price. The need for haste and secrecy that had prompted the OSS and the FBI break-ins of *Amerasia*'s offices obviated requests for search warrants. Consequently a court might not allow the material gathered during the break-ins to be used as evidence. Even the classified documents found during the arrests of those involved might not be allowed as evidence because the arrests stemmed from the earlier warrantless searches. This trade-off between the need quickly to stem the loss of sensitive information and the much slower pace required to gather evidence that could be used in a criminal proceeding plagued espionage cases throughout the cold war.

There were other complications as well. If *Amerasia* had been the cover for a Japanese or Nazi espionage operation, the government would have struck with a heavy hand. But *Amerasia* was Communist aligned. The journal itself was a product of the Popular Front era, founded and funded in 1936 by two wealthy patrons of the Communist party, Frederick Vanderbilt Field and Philip Jaffe. Field was a scion of the prominent Vanderbilt family while Jaffe was a frequent social associate of Soviet diplomats. Given these connections, Secretary Forrestal feared that a full-scale prosecution of *Amerasia* would publicize the threat of

Communist espionage and embarrass President Roosevelt in his dealings with the Soviet Union in the final stages of World War II.

The 1945 arrest of John Service, a professional diplomat with White House connections, was also a problem. The FBI secretly recorded (without a warrant) a meeting between Service and Jaffe where Service briefed Jaffe about U.S. policy toward China and passed on reports highly embarrassing to the government of Chiang Kai-shek. In retrospect it seems that Service was not engaged in espionage on behalf of the Soviet Union, as were some of the others in the *Amerasia* case. Rather, Service was improperly leaking government information that he hoped *Amerasia* would use to influence American foreign policy. Convinced that the Chiang regime was doomed because of its corruption and incompetence, he wanted the United States to establish friendly relations with the Chinese Communists, then poised to resume a civil war with Chiang. Service had the support of some high administration officials who disagreed with President Roosevelt's pro-Chiang policy. One of those was Lauchlin Currie, an influential White House aide, who feared that the activities of anti-Chiang advocates inside the government, including his own, would become public if the *Amerasia* case went forward.

Currie procured for Service the legal assistance of Thomas Corcoran. A former leading official of the New Deal administration in the 1930s, Corcoran by 1945 had become one of the most influential lobbyists and "fixers" in Washington. One of his major clients was Chiang's Nationalist government, the government that Service opposed—but Corcoran also wanted to do a favor for Currie. Corcoran was a highly successful lobbyist because he performed tasks such as this and was owed favors by influential government officials. He pressured the Justice Department to go easy on Service, calling in his important political "chips" with Attorney General Tom Clark and his chief aides. Corcoran's pressure, fear of handing the Republicans an exploitable scandal, and the possibility that a judge would disallow evidence gathered from warrantless searches led the Justice

Department to retreat from its plan to indict those in the *Amerasia* case for espionage.

Instead the Justice Department dropped its actions against Service, Gayn, and Mitchell and indicted Jaffe, Roth, and Larsen only for unlawful possession of government documents. With this lesser charge, no mention need be made in open court of communism, the Soviet Union, or any controversial matter. But even here much of the evidence, while conclusive, was questionably admissible in court. Further, even though espionage was not mentioned, the case might still become a political embarrassment at a particularly vulnerable time: President Roosevelt had just died and President Truman was struggling for control of the administration. With these factors in mind, prosecutors moved for a quick plea bargain. Larsen and Jaffe agreed to guilty verdicts in exchange for fines and no jail time. Larsen was also fired from his State Department post. Roth had in the meantime been discharged from the navy, and his case was dropped entirely.

While the leakage of classified documents through *Amerasia* was stopped, the case left a harvest of suspicion and frustration. Because none of the arrests resulted in a contested trial with the presentation of evidence, and because the Justice Department played down the importance of the case, only slowly was it revealed that hundreds of classified documents had been stolen from the State Department. When this information finally surfaced, Republicans saw it as a cover-up (which it was) and used the incident to illustrate the administration's laxity on security matters. The administration responded to the partisan attack with a partisan defense—that everything had been handled properly, that there was no espionage and no scandal. When rumors of manipulation of the Justice Department on Service's behalf reached Republicans, through leaks from angry FBI and OSS officials, they were even more convinced that a spy scandal was being hushed up.

The competing interpretations of and myths about the *Amerasia* case followed a pattern that occurred often during the postwar period. The Republican/conservative view saw the case, at best, as a scandalous example of the Democratic administration's woefully lax security and indifference toward security violations involving Communists, or, at worst, of high-level toleration of or even involvement in Communist espionage and treachery. In part this view was sincerely held, but it also contained a strong element of partisanship that saw the *Amerasia* case as an exploitable tool against the incumbent Democrats. Republican supporters of America First in 1940–1941 had seen their anti-intervention policy depicted by Democrats as pro-Hitler and fifth columnist. In 1945 and 1946 they struck back by linking the Democratic administration to *Amerasia* espionage and by blurring John Service's discreditable leaking with spying.

On the Democratic/liberal side the interpretations of the *Amerasia* case were more diverse and presaged what would become a split in liberalism between the Popular Front views of the 1930s and the emerging anti-Communist liberalism of the post–World War II era. The Popular Front liberal view was that those implicated in the *Amerasia* case were heroic figures innocent of any wrongdoing and victimized by irrational anti-Communist hysteria or framed by the FBI. In this and in other cases, Popular Front spokesmen dismissed any evidence, such as the hundreds of classified documents found in Philip Jaffe's office, as forged, faked, planted by the FBI, and in any case insignificant. The anti-Communist liberal position, still a minority view in Democratic circles in 1945, condemned the security breach involved in the *Amerasia* case and saw those involved as rogues who got away lightly. Anti-Communist liberals, however, were Democrats and resented Republican use of the issue to taint the New Deal. Because of the threat that Republicans could use this and other cases to discredit the entire Roosevelt heritage, anti-Communist liberals tended to minimize the extent to which the Popular Front mentality of the 1930s and early 1940s had affected the Roosevelt administration and the extent to which *Amerasia* was the consequence of an attitude that regarded Communists and liberals as part of a common enterprise.

The Truman administration's treatment of the episode was a partisan defensive crouch that in public trivialized the issue in order to deflect partisan Republican attack. In private, however, the president was irritated by the *Amerasia* case, and it contributed to his decision to increase security requirements for federal employees.

On the heels of the *Amerasia* case came that of Igor Gouzenko. Gouzenko, a lieutenant in Soviet military intelligence, was a cipher clerk at the Soviet embassy in Canada from June 1943 until his defection in September 1945 with his pregnant wife and a young son. When he defected he brought along a batch of Soviet intelligence reports and his memory of the messages he had been encoding and decoding between the embassy's intelligence officers and their Moscow superiors. His information showed that the Soviets had been operating an extensive espionage apparatus in Canada at a time when Canada was an ally of the Soviet Union, using personnel provided by the Canadian Communist party. Gouzenko's documents initiated an espionage investigation that led to the imprisonment of eight Canadians, including Fred Rose, a Communist member of the Canadian parliament; Sam Carr, organizing secretary of the Communist Party of Canada; and Dr. Allan Nunn May, a nuclear scientist.

What made this Canadian affair a matter of intense American interest was May's involvement in the joint American-British-Canadian atomic bomb project. Gouzenko's information indicated that intelligence operations out of the Soviet embassy in Ottawa had been just a branch of a much larger Soviet espionage effort aimed at penetration of American and British high-technology weapons programs. British security officers and the American FBI pursued Gouzenko's leads, and in both nations several scientists and engineers on sensitive projects were implicated in Soviet spying.

Gouzenko's information also assisted a super-secret American code-breaking project labeled Venona. In a major intelligence coup, American cryptographers in the late 1940s and 1950s partially decoded some 2,200 coded cables dating from 1942 to 1946 sent by Soviet diplomatic offices in the United States to Moscow, including messages from Soviet intelligence officers operating from these Soviet diplomatic missions. The Soviets had used a code they believed to be unbreakable, but American cryptographers discovered that the Soviets had made technical errors that allowed the breaking of some of the coded messages. Not until 1995 did the U.S. government begin releasing the Venona intercepts. These decoded cables, whose existence before 1995 was only rumored, indicated that about two hundred Americans, many of them American Communist party members, were working for Soviet intelligence as spies.

Until the cold war ended American counterintelligence officials were adamant that the code-breaking success of Venona could not be revealed to the Soviets. Consequently the evidence of spying provided by Venona could not be used in criminal court cases against Soviet spies. Thus in a number of cases where other sufficient evidence could not be found to bring a criminal charge, the identified spies were quietly eased out of military-related work. Although this was the only sensible course, it left security officials highly frustrated that persons they knew to be Soviet spies were allowed to go free. Sometimes the frustration resulted in leaks to Republicans of information about the spies who were allowed to go quietly. Often the leak suggested or was interpreted to be more evidence of a deliberate cover-up of espionage.

In 1948 the FBI discovered one reason why it had had only limited success in its efforts to expose Soviet spies. By this time the FBI was convinced that a number of its operations to uncover Soviet intelligence rings were being leaked to the Soviets, allowing those involved to cease their activity, destroy records, and frustrate FBI attempts to gather sufficient evidence to bring criminal charges. Based on information gleaned from Venona's partially decoded Soviet cable messages between Moscow and Soviet diplomatic offices in the United States, the FBI began surveillance of certain government employees who had access to information about FBI counterintelligence operations. Late in 1948 it traced the leak to Judith Coplon in the Justice Department's Foreign Agents Registration Division, an office that worked with FBI counterintelligence. Early in 1949 Coplon was caught handing over files on FBI operations to a Soviet diplomat. To their embarrassment, government security officials discovered that when the Justice Department hired Coplon in 1944, a security check had turned up evidence of her Communist sympathies. At that time most security officials concerned themselves with fascist sympathies, and her Communist links were ignored. Coplon was tried and convicted, but on appeal her conviction was overturned on a technicality that disallowed use of most of the evidence against her. The evidence, though ultimately inadmissible in court, was overwhelming in proving she was a Soviet spy. The fact that a demonstrably guilty spy could use the elaborate rules of the American judicial system to escape justice added to the public's frustration and the suspicion that incumbent government officials were disinclined or incompetent to deal with Communist-related security matters.

Perhaps most upsetting to the American public was the exposure of Soviet atomic spying. Gouzenko's information and partial decoding of Soviet cable traffic pointed security officials toward a senior British nuclear scientist, Klaus Fuchs. When confronted, Fuchs revealed he had been a Communist party member in his native Germany before fleeing the Nazis, and confessed to providing the Soviets extensive information on his work in building the atomic bomb at Los Alamos. A British court sent Fuchs to prison for fourteen years.

In his confession Fuchs described an American contact that the FBI soon identified as Harry Gold. Gold had been named in 1947 as a Soviet agent by Elizabeth Bentley, herself a former Soviet spy. But Gold had not been indicted because of the lack of collaborative evidence to support Bentley's story. In 1947 Gold had withstood FBI questioning, confident that it had little to back up Bentley's accusation. This time, however, Fuchs's information implicated Gold in atomic espionage, a far more serious matter than Bentley's information of his involvement in low-level industrial spying.

Hoping that his cooperation would allow him to avoid the maximum penalty (execution) under American law, Gold confessed. He not only confirmed he had been a courier between Fuchs in Los Alamos and a Soviet intelligence officer, he also provided a description of a second Los Alamos source, a soldier from whom he had couriered information. Using Gold's confession, the FBI shortly thereafter confronted David Greenglass, who had been a soldier working at the Los Alamos atomic facility. Greenglass also confessed. His confession implicated his brother-in-law, Julius Rosenberg, in Soviet atomic espionage.

Greenglass's sister, Ethel, had met Julius Rosenberg while he was studying electrical engineering at the City College of New York in the mid-1930s. Both became activists in the Young Communist League and later adult members of the Communist party. (Julius recruited the younger David Greenglass into the Young Communist League.) In 1943 the Rosenbergs dropped out of open Communist activity and into Soviet espionage. Julius coordinated an espionage ring that consisted largely of engineers with Communist backgrounds like himself who worked on military technology projects. When he learned in 1944 that his brother-in-law had been assigned to Los Alamos, he asked Greenglass to provide information on his work to the Soviet Union. Greenglass agreed and later provided information about the bomb mechanisms he worked on as a soldier/machinist, particularly the high-explosive lens that initiated the atomic chain reaction.

When Greenglass's arrest was announced in the press, Morton Sobell, a Rosenberg engineering friend who had worked on military radar, fled to Mexico but was seized by Mexican authorities and returned to the United States. Also disappearing from the United States were two other of Rosenberg's engineer friends, Joel Barr and Alfred Sarant. Both reappeared many decades later as engineers working on military electronics in the Soviet Union. They told Western reporters they had left home to avoid anti-Communist hysteria and had never been involved in espionage.

Convicting the Rosenbergs was not a difficult task for the prosecution. The testimony of Harry Gold and David Greenglass was supported by a mass of collaborative evidence. Nor was the Rosenbergs' defense able to discredit the prosecution's evidence or to present a convincing alternative to the prosecution's case. Both Rosenbergs were convicted and in 1953 were executed. Morton Sobell, tried with the Rosenbergs, was also convicted and received a thirty-year sentence. Gold and Greenglass were imprisoned but given lighter sentences because of their cooperation with the prosecution.

The evidence that the Rosenbergs were involved in Soviet espionage was overwhelming and has only grown over time. In 1995 the release of the Venona intercepts further confirmed the accuracy of the government's case. Among those definitively named as spies by these decoded Soviet messages were the Rosenbergs, Klaus Fuchs, David Greenglass, Morton Sobell, Joel Barr, and Alfred Sarant.

The most debatable aspect of the Rosenberg case was the decision to execute Ethel Rosenberg. Each of the major advances in this case had been made possible by participants talking. First Gouzenko defected and talked, which led to Fuchs. His confession led to Harry Gold. Gold confessed, and this led to David Greenglass. Greenglass's confession led to the Rosenbergs and Sobell. Here, however, the chain stopped. Neither Julius Rosenberg nor Sobell would cooperate with the authorities. Joel Barr and Alfred Sarant, of course, avoided involvement in the case by secretly fleeing to the USSR. The FBI had information implicating others in the Soviet spy ring of which Julius Rosenberg was a key figure, and intensely questioned several. None, however, confessed or was tried for espionage because of insufficient evidence. One of them, William Perl, an aeronautical engineer, was convicted of perjury for lying to a grand jury about his activities. (The Venona intercepts also confirm Perl's espionage.)

Because the government had evidence that Julius Rosenberg was part of a much broader Soviet operation, it sought to pressure him into cooperating and providing evidence against others. It applied that pressure through Ethel Rosenberg. Her arrest and trial were in large part driven by the desire to force Julius to tell what he knew about other Soviet operations. The evidence was convincing that Ethel Rosenberg had assisted her husband in espionage, but her role was not as central as Julius's. Nonetheless the prosecution treated her as a full partner in her husband's crimes. Judge Irving Kaufman, who presided over the trial, consulted the prosecution privately about the sentence. His decision to execute Ethel appears to have been coordinated with the government's continued effort to force the Rosenbergs to cooperate. Up to their execution both were told that cooperation would bring an immediate stay and a reconsideration of their sentences. Both the Rosenbergs, however, were deeply committed Communists. They refused cooperation and went to their deaths claiming their complete innocence and even denying they were Communists. While there was no reasonable doubt of Ethel's guilt, execution seemed excessive considering the extent of her involvement in carrying out espionage. The government's decision to use the threat of her execution to pressure Julius, and then following through on the threat when the pressure failed, was gruesome.

Defenders of the Rosenbergs mounted an active publicity campaign after their conviction, a campaign that grew with their execution. Communist parties around the world treated the Rosenbergs as martyrs. In general, defenders took the line that the evidence against the Rosenbergs was manufactured by the FBI and that Gold, Greenglass, and others who provided damaging testimony had lied voluntarily or had been blackmailed by the FBI. Although during their trial the Rosenbergs had presented themselves as nonpolitical, in the posttrial defense campaigns they called themselves "progressives," but not Communists, who supported "peace" and who had been framed by a government seeking to discredit all who believed in peace. Later the Rosenbergs' defenders added the charge that Julius and Ethel were executed because they were Jewish, seeking to offset news of Stalin's instigation of anti-Semitic purges throughout Eastern Europe.

The Rosenberg public defense was a highly emotional one, making major use of the pathetic sight of the young sons left orphaned by the twin executions. The letters exchanged between Julius and Ethel as they awaited execution were also highly publicized. The two were deeply committed to each other, and the letters have considerable emotional appeal. Ethel's particularly also are infused with revolutionary ideology. Confident that communism was historically destined to conquer the earth, in one letter she savored her eventual revenge, writing: "Wait, wait and tremble, ye mad masters, this barbarism, this infamy you practice upon us, and with which you regale yourselves presently, will not go unanswered, unavenged, forever! The whirlwind gathers, before which you must fly like the chaff!" The winds of history, as it turned out, did not blow as Ethel thought they would. After the collapse of communism in Eastern Europe in 1989–1991, monuments to the Rosenbergs that had been erected during the Communist era were quietly put away.

In recent decades many historians have suggested that while the Soviet intelligence services recruited some American Communists for espionage, this did not directly involve the American Communist party. They have asserted that the pervasive belief in the late 1940s and 1950s that the CPUSA directly assisted Soviet spying was false, a product of anti-Communist hysteria. In this view, American Communists were unfairly persecuted for the sins of the Soviet intelligence services. Since the collapse of Soviet communism, however, documents found in Soviet archives as well as the Venona intercepts confirm the CPUSA's direct involvement in Soviet espionage.

Although the chief Soviet intelligence archives remain closed, documents found in other archives prove that Jay Lovestone, general secretary (head) of the CPUSA in the late 1920s, and Earl Browder, general secretary of the party from 1932 to 1945, both recruited Americans to spy for the Soviet Union. Other documents show that Eugene Dennis, general secretary of the party from 1945 to 1959, during World War II supervised Communist penetration of America's wartime intelligence agency, the Office of Strategic Services, and its wartime propaganda arm, the Office of War Information. Most relevant to the postwar spate of espionage cases are documents directly linking the CPUSA to atomic espionage. These documents confirm that the CPUSA's underground worked directly with and for the Soviet intelligence officer Vasily Zubilin, who supervised the Soviet theft of atomic bomb secrets.

The collapse of the Soviet Union has also brought out information about two other American Communists. Anotoli

Yatskov and other retired Soviet intelligence officers credited
Morris and Lona Cohen as having played a key role in Soviet
penetration of the Manhattan project. Morris Cohen was cited as
recruiting an unnamed American physicist who was a major
source of Soviet information; Lona was praised as a courier to a
Soviet source at Los Alamos. That the Cohens were Soviet spies
was not a revelation. In the mid-1950s the Cohens had showed
up in London using fraudulent New Zealand passports and
working quietly as rare book dealers. In 1961 British police arrested the Cohens when it rolled up a Soviet spy ring that had
penetrated the British admiralty; British police found the ring's
radio and microfilming equipment in the Cohens' residence.
The two were convicted of espionage and imprisoned but in 1967
were exchanged for a British spy held by the Soviets. The Cohens then retired to Moscow to live on pensions provided by the
Soviet intelligence services.

That the Cohens had been involved in espionage in the United
States before their appearance in Britain had long been suspected. The two had disappeared from New York at the time the
Rosenbergs were arrested, and the FBI had turned up evidence
leading them to suspect that the Cohens were somehow linked to
the Rosenbergs. But until the Soviet Union collapsed, this had all
been only suspicion. Yatskov and other retired Soviet officers
praised Morris Cohen for his major role in stealing the secrets of
the atomic bomb. Cohen, who had joined the CPUSA in 1935, was
one of several thousand American Communists who fought with
the International Brigades in the Spanish Civil War. According
to Yatskov and others, Cohen had been recruited as a Soviet
agent while recuperating from wounds in Spain. In turn, he recruited Lona after his return to the United States.

It is difficult to overestimate the importance of the Fuchs and
Rosenberg cases in arousing anti-Communist sentiment. America's monopoly of the atomic bomb in 1945 appeared to give the
United States a war-winning weapon that guaranteed American
security. The Soviet explosion of a nuclear bomb of its own in
1949 destroyed that sense of physical security. The United States
had gone through two world wars without suffering serious

civilian deaths or destruction; now it faced a ruthless dictator with weapons that could destroy whole cities in one blow. Further, the nation's leaders had not prepared Americans for the Soviet bomb. Officials had assured Americans that it would be a decade at least and probably more before any possible adversary developed atomic weapons. When the Fuchs and Rosenberg cases broke and showed that the Soviets had stolen the secrets of the atomic bomb with the help of American Communists, the American public was furious and wanted drastic punishment of those responsible.

In retrospect, given Stalin's commitment to develop atomic weapons and the skill of Russian scientists, it probably would not have taken the Soviets a decade to develop a bomb. Espionage, however, saved the Soviet Union several years and an immense amount of money because it was able to skip much of the expensive development stage of the bomb project. The additional expense and added years and uncertainty of building an atomic bomb without espionage would have been a major burden to the Soviet Union and restrained Stalin's foreign policy objectives. It is unlikely, for example, that he would have approved North Korea's invasion of South Korea in 1950 had the American atomic monopoly still existed. Without the threat of Soviet atomic retaliation, American use of or even the threat to use nuclear weapons could have stopped the North Korean invasion in its tracks.

In the minds of most Americans, these spy cases and others indelibly linked the American Communist party to Soviet espionage. Most Americans came to view the CPUSA as a sort of fifth column, combining espionage with political subversion, a view that revived in a slightly modified form attitudes first formed during the time of the Nazi-Soviet pact. And most Americans thought the new Communist fifth column should be treated in the same fashion as the Nazi/fascist fifth-column threat of the late 1930s and early 1940s.

4

The House Committee on
Un-American Activities

BEYOND SOVIET ESPIONAGE, public alarm over communism was heightened by revelations from the House Committee
on Un-American Activities, more commonly known as HUAC,
or the House Un-American Activities Committee. HUAC began
in the 1930s as the Special Committee on Un-American Activity,
with its principal focus on American fascism and Nazism. It
would not have been created but for the work of Representative
Samuel Dickstein, a liberal Democrat from New York. The
committee was popularly known as the McCormack-Dickstein
Committee after its chairman, Representative John McCormack
(Democrat, Massachusetts), and its dominant member, Dickstein. All the virtues and vices that would later mark post–World
War II congressional investigations of communism were first
played out by Dickstein's investigations of domestic fascism.

The McCormack-Dickstein Committee focused public attention on the growth of Nazi and quasi-fascist movements and
helped to develop a popular antifascist constituency. That American fascism never became a significant threat to American
democracy, only a potential one, ought to be credited in part to
the work of Samuel Dickstein. There was, however, a price for
this success. Dickstein did not conduct a calm, dispassionate examination of a potential subversive threat but rather launched a
crusade against what he perceived as a menacing evil. He exag-

gerated the right-wing extremist threat far beyond its modest size (claiming that "you can find almost 200,000 men of the [German-American] Bund ready to put on uniforms and to use a gun"), exaggerated the extent of links between domestic fascists and Berlin (contending, erroneously as it turned out, that Hitler was sending millions of dollars to finance subversion in America), and asserted a threat of espionage, sabotage, and violence that was more possibility than probability. Dickstein coerced witnesses to explain their political and racial beliefs and reconcile those beliefs with mainstream ideas of American patriotism; he then critiqued and condemned those answers he didn't like. Uncooperative witnesses were insulted and subjected to verbal abuse and lectures about their moral shortcomings. Dickstein believed that exposure was the most effective weapon against domestic Nazis. When Chairman McCormack insisted that names and testimony remain secret because they were unverified, Dickstein simply picked out the most sensational parts and inserted them in the *Congressional Record* on his own authority, naming various individuals as "spies" or "Nazi aides." In some cases entirely innocent persons had their reputations damaged and their lives ruined by false accusations from overzealous or irresponsible antifascist witnesses.

Dickstein was not personally popular with his colleagues. He was a highly liberal New Dealer in a House that by 1938 was growing less friendly to the Roosevelt administration. When he asked the House to continue the temporary McCormack-Dickstein Committee as a special committee to investigate "un-American propaganda of religious, racial or subversive political prejudices," the House turned down his resolution. Dickstein then allied himself to Representative Martin Dies, a conservative Texas Democrat who was more popular with the House. Sponsored by Dies, the resolution passed. But the House Democratic leadership got its revenge by excluding Dickstein from the committee. Martin Dies became its chairman and dominant figure, and the committee was popularly called the Dies Committee.

In his investigations Dies took the path blazed by Dickstein rather than by the restrained John McCormack: exaggeration (he

more than doubled Dickstein's already ridiculous figure of
200,000 fascists and warned of 480,000 Nazis active in the United
States), minimal concern for documentation, abuse of uncooperative witnesses, and seeking the sensational. Also he initially pursued domestic Nazis and extremist anti-Semites, and increased
press interest in the hearings by producing witnesses who testified that the German-American Bund encouraged sexual per-
missiveness, including homosexuality, as well as Nazi ideology.
Dies quickly opened a second front against domestic communism, a matter of minor concern to Dickstein. Although he
would continue to harass the extremist right (Dies exposed the
bizarre plans of retired General George Moseley and George
Deatherage of the anti-Semitic Knights of the White Camellia to
organize a private army), Dies put major emphasis on the extremist left.

In taking on domestic communism, Dies had more in his
sights than the Communist party itself. Dies was one of a sizable
group of Democratic conservatives, mostly from the rural South
and West, who had become disenchanted with Roosevelt's presidency and resented the domination of the Democratic party
by the New Deal coalition of urban liberals, organized labor,
Jews, blacks, Catholics, and Eastern European ethnics. Dies
hoped to weaken the broader liberal coalition by tainting the entire enterprise with communism. Some conservatives regarded
communism and liberalism as part of an ideological continuum,
seeing liberals as moderate Communists or Communists as liberals in a hurry. To these conservatives, insisting that the broader
liberal movement was by its nature accommodating to Communists was to point out an ideological truth. Many conservatives,
however, simply found it a polemical convenience to taint liberalism with communism.

Dies sought to use his investigations to affect elections and influence legislation. In the fall of 1938 he held highly publicized
hearings about Communist infiltration of Minnesota's Farmer-
Labor party, a pro-Roosevelt state-level third party that dominated Minnesota politics at the time. The charges, though true,
were levied in sensational fashion and with deliberate intent to

influence the upcoming state elections. In that election the incumbent governor, Elmer Benson, a Farmer-Laborite who worked closely with Communists, went down to a landslide defeat, and the Farmer-Labor party lost its control of Minnesota's congressional delegation and the state house of representatives.

Dies's influence in this election should not be exaggerated. Benson had faced a challenge in the Farmer-Labor party primary from a former Farmer-Labor governor, Hjalmar Petersen, who made his opposition to Benson's allowing Communists into the Farmer-Labor party a major primary issue. Benson barely defeated Petersen, only to see the same issue taken up by the Republican gubernatorial candidate, Harold Stassen. Benson, while an able orator, was an inept politician who had deeply alienated major sections of the Farmer-Labor constituency. Stassen, in contrast, was a superb campaigner and political tactician.

The Dies Committee also investigated Communist infiltration of the Federal Theatre Project, a New Deal program that provided work relief for unemployed actors and theatrical personnel by financing low-cost or free plays. While most of the productions of the Federal Theatre Project were standard classics, it also staged many experimental plays and commissioned new works. Some of these new plays were propagandistic in tone and reflected the liberal and radical sentiments of many of the actors and playwrights. The Dies hearings were sensationalist and exaggerated. Had the Federal Theatre Project enjoyed solid congressional support before Dies's attacks, it could have survived. But Congress wanted to cut the New Deal's relief programs somewhere, and the theater project was among the most unpopular of them. Dies's hearings were merely the final blow. Roosevelt concluded the program couldn't be saved and acquiesced to Congress killing it.

Dies's harassment of the Roosevelt administration and his attempts to portray it as seriously infiltrated by Communists greatly annoyed President Roosevelt and liberals. Many liberals believed that Dies's professed hostility toward fascism was false and that he was a secret Nazi. In hopes of discrediting the congressman, in 1940 Gardner Jackson, a mid-level New Deal offi-

cial, paid cash to David Mayne, an official of the quasi-fascist Silver Shirts, and promised him a government job in return for letters linking Dies to William Dudley Pelley, chief of the Silver
Shirts and would-be American *Führer.* On the basis of the letters,
The Nation magazine and Representative Frank Hook of Michigan, a liberal Democrat, demanded the disbanding of the Dies
committee. There is every reason to believe that Jackson, Hook,
and *The Nation* were sincere, but their dislike of Dies had weakened their critical faculties. There were no ties between Pelley
and Dies: Mayne had forged the letters to get Jackson's money,
and Dies quickly exposed Mayne's fabrication. Hook was forced
to apologize, and Mayne pleaded guilty to a fraud charge. Dies
emerged from this episode stronger than ever and looking like
the target of a smear campaign.

The period of the Nazi-Soviet pact was ideal for Dies; the nation experienced a mild panic about Nazi or Communist fifth-
column threats, and Dies could flail away at either with
assurance of media coverage. Once the United States entered the
war, however, Dies faced frustration. While he and his committee continued to harass and expose domestic fascists and Nazis,
Congress no longer played a central role. The Roosevelt administration created a large wartime security apparatus that investigated, prosecuted, and suppressed pro-Nazi, pro-fascist, and
pro-Japanese organizations and activists. Dies was equally frustrated on the Communist issue because of public indifference.
After the Nazi attack on the Soviet Union, Communists shifted
to an aggressive anti-Nazi stance and fully supported America's
war effort. The great sacrifices made by the peoples of the Soviet
Union in resisting Hitler's invasion won much sympathy and admiration from Americans. Although public dislike of communism remained pervasive, for most Americans it had become a
tertiary issue when compared with the war against Nazi Germany, fascist Italy, and imperial Japan.

In part due to his frustration, but due as well to ill health and
the prospect of a tough reelection campaign, in 1944 Dies retired.
His committee left a mixed legacy. Despite Dies's misuse of the
facts or his sometimes confused interpretations, his information

was accurate more often than his enemies would concede. The Dies Committee research director, J. B. Matthews, knew Communists well from his years in the 1930s as one of the nation's most prominent "fellow-travelers." Dies and Matthews were right on three central points: American Communists were conspirators, did act as agents for the Soviet Union, and ardently sought to subvert America's constitutional and democratic order—this at a time when a large segment of American liberals admired Stalin and thought that Communists were native American radicals who believed in the nation's democratic traditions. Their accuracy on these points, however, was obscured by Dies's desire to use the Communist issue to discredit the New Deal and their exaggerated view that Communists had penetrated all of American liberalism rather than being only a part of a broad and otherwise democratic New Deal coalition.

Martin Dies retired on the eve of what was to be an era of surging popular anticommunism as the events of the postwar era mobilized one latent anti-Communist constituency after another. Although Democratic House leaders planned to use the occasion of Dies's retirement to disband his committee, John Rankin (Democrat, Mississippi) put together a coalition of conservative Democrats and Republicans to reconstitute it as the permanent House Committee on Un-American Activities. Rankin could have taken the chairmanship of HUAC, but he was already chairman of the Veterans Affairs Committee, a high-profile and powerful committee at the end of World War II. He chose to keep the chairmanship of Veterans Affairs and allow the House leadership to install a weak chairman for HUAC. Rankin was, however, a member of HUAC and dominated it by controlling a majority coalition of conservative Democrats and Republicans.

John Rankin was easily the most malicious man ever to control the House Un-American Activities Committee. He was an ardent racist who believed that the darker races were genetically consigned to an inferior status and who announced more than once that slavery had been a blessing for American blacks. His chief hatred, however, was reserved for Jews. He saw the New Deal, communism, and the movement for racial equality as Jewish plots. To Rankin, anticommunism was a tool to be used to expose the New Deal and liberalism as a Jewish conspiracy. Communism in itself was not of great interest to Rankin unless he could connect it to Jews. With Rankin dominating HUAC, its actions in 1945 and 1946 gave satisfaction chiefly to anti-Semites who shared Rankin's views and to Republicans who took pleasure in having a Democratic committee bashing the New Deal.

In the 1946 elections Republicans gained control of the House and made J. Parnell Thomas of New Jersey chairman of HUAC. The House Un-American Activities Committee under Thomas was more effective than it had been under either Dies or Rankin. Although Thomas had only a shallow understanding of communism, he was a more consistent and responsible leader than Dies and did not share Rankin's raging hatred of Jews. Thomas also hired a new chief counsel, Robert Stripling, who provided HUAC with its most effective staff support ever. A freshman Republican member of the House Un-American Activities Committee, Richard Nixon of California, added to the committee majority a politically astute and sophisticated intelligence.

HUAC under Republican leadership made its first foray into the public eye with an investigation of Hollywood. In the 1930s the political preferences of people in the movie industry had covered the entire range but leaned strongly to the liberal and left side of the spectrum. Inside the liberal/left Hollywood community was a lively Communist presence centered on several dozen screenwriters who were active party members. These Communist screenwriters helped to found and for many years controlled the Screen Writers Guild. Communists were also active in a number of other movie industry unions and dominated the leadership of the Conference of Studio Unions (CSU), an alliance of unions of various movie industry crafts. Some actors and actresses were Communists, but only a very few stars joined the party. A larger number were enthusiastic Popular Front liberals.

Hollywood Communists succeeded in raising a great deal of money for political and social causes approved by the Communist party and in guiding a number of Hollywood big names into Popular Front causes. But that was about the extent of Communist success. Communist screenwriters and actors tried but had little success in injecting their ideology into movies. Of the many hundreds of films produced in the heyday of the Hollywood Reds, only a handful contain significant Communist propaganda. The movie *Mission to Moscow* defended Stalin's purges, and *Song of Russia* portrayed the USSR as a bucolic paradise. Both, however, were products more of the atmosphere of the 1942–1945 Soviet-American military alliance than of manipulation by movie industry Communists.

Even before HUAC arrived in Hollywood, Communists in the industry had taken several rude blows. In 1945 the Communist-led Conference of Studio Unions launched an industry-wide strike. Not only were studio heads opposed to the CSU, but its bid for leadership over the industry's chaotic labor relations was contested by the AFL's International Alliance of Theatrical Stage Employees, led by Roy Brewer, a strong anti-Communist. Brewer arranged an alliance with the powerful Teamsters union, broke the CSU strike, and established his International Alliance of Theatrical Stage Employees as Hollywood's predominant union. At the same time a liberal but anti-Communist faction under the leadership of Ronald Reagan took control of Hollywood's chief "glamour" union, the Screen Actors Guild, from a Popular Front faction with a strong Communist presence.

HUAC's hearings into communism in Hollywood opened with newspaper and radio coverage that dwarfed media attention paid to more typical HUAC hearings. The initial witnesses were actors and industry officials hostile to the Communist party. Actors George Murphy (later U.S. senator from California) and Ronald Reagan (later California's governor and president of the United States) made informative and calm statements about the attempts of Communists to control the Screen Actors Guild.

Others, with prompting from the congressmen, made lengthy and tedious denunciations of communism. Easily the most memorable line came from Gary Cooper, one of the stars of the era. Cooper said he didn't know much about communism, but from what he did know, "It isn't on the level." One could not have

asked for an answer that better fitted Cooper's screen persona as
the strong, silent, red-blooded American male. In his testimony
Jack Warner of Warner Brothers Studios showed a film industry
executive at his ingratiating worst. Warner, whose company had
produced the pro-Stalin film *Mission to Moscow* and was a bit on
the defensive, proclaimed his Americanism in exaggerated and
florid tones, volunteered that he would fire any Communists
who worked for him, offered to pay the passage to Russia of
American Communists, and pledged to produce anti-Communist films. Warner's testimony showed that he and other studio
owners were deadly afraid of adverse publicity.

When HUAC arrived at unfriendly witnesses, the result was
even more spectacular. All of those called as unfriendly witnesses
were close to the Communist party and most were, in fact, secret
members. They had faithfully followed the Communist party in
every shift in its policy, hailed Stalin as a great and wise leader,
cheered the Soviet purges in which millions were murdered, favored an aggressive U.S. anti-Nazi policy until the Nazi-Soviet
pact, opposed American aid to those fighting Hitler during the
period of the Nazi-Soviet pact, and then returned to an anti-
Nazi policy once Germany attacked the Soviet Union.

On the advice of the Communist party, most of the unfriendly
witnesses took a defiant stand toward the committee. They denied HUAC's right to question them and stated that HUAC was
"preparing a Fascist America" with Nazi-style concentration
camps. Very quickly, the unfriendly witnesses and HUAC congressmen were screaming at each other and trading abusive remarks. When the hearings ended, Congress cited ten of the
unfriendly witnesses for contempt of Congress for refusing to
answer questions. Of the ten, nine were party members and the
tenth a close ally.

The "Hollywood Ten," as they were known, could have
avoided contempt charges by invoking their right under the
Fifth Amendment to the Constitution to refuse to give testimony
that might be used against them in a criminal case. But invoking
the Fifth implied that they had something incriminating to hide.
Instead of the Fifth Amendment right, the ten claimed they had

a free-speech First Amendment right to refuse to answer questions. Federal courts, however, maintained that the right of Congress to subpoena witnesses and compel testimony was well established; in the absence of a Fifth Amendment claim, the defendants had no grounds to refuse to satisfy the subpoena. The ten went to prison for short periods for their defiance. One of them, Ring Lardner, Jr., served his time in prison alongside of J. Parnell Thomas, HUAC's chairman. Thomas's role subjected him to unusual scrutiny, and journalists discovered that Thomas was padding his congressional expense accounts and taking salary kickbacks from his staff. The revelation led to Thomas's trial and imprisonment.

Hollywood's Communists were already in retreat in 1947, but the publicity given the HUAC hearings turned the retreat into a panicky rout. Hollywood's Communists had expected that the broader liberal and Popular Front community would provide them with cover. Initially a number of major stars and some studio executives did attack the committee and make a free-speech defense of the Hollywood Ten. But this did not last long. The general public was becoming increasingly aroused by the Soviet threat, and evidence that the unfriendly witnesses were enthusiastic supporters of Stalin did not go over well. Nor did the Hollywood Ten win sympathy with their refusal to answer questions and their denunciation of America as a fascist nation. In an industry as sensitive as Hollywood was to the whims of public opinion, the message was clear: association with communism was a potential threat to the box office. Visible support for the Hollywood Ten melted away. Studio executives made it clear that actors, actresses, screenwriters, and directors who were Communists and who did not repudiate their allegiances would not be employed in the industry.

The hearings failed to show that Hollywood's Reds had inserted a significant amount of propaganda into films, and Chairman Thomas's hope that the hearings would generate support for some type of censorship of the movies went unrewarded. But the hearings were by political standards a huge success because of the intense publicity they received. Accordingly, HUAC found reasons to return to the movie industry in 1951. Mindful of the fate of the Hollywood Ten, this time Hollywood's remaining Communists invoked the Fifth Amendment and legally refused to answer questions. Although frustrating HUAC's attempts to elicit additional information, this tactic confirmed in the minds of most of the public that these witnesses were Communists.

Those Hollywood Communists who invoked the Fifth Amendment escaped legal penalty but nonetheless paid a price. The major studios had publicly pledged not to employ Communists, and these "Fifth Amendment Communists" (most were or had been party members) fell under the ban. Until the late 1950s the major movie studios and radio and television networks maintained an informal blacklist that excluded Communists from employment. The number of persons blacklisted in the movie industry was between two hundred and three hundred, with perhaps an equal number in radio, television, and other segments of the entertainment industry. Even if studio executives had not created an informal blacklist, market considerations alone would have discouraged employment of screen actors and actresses who were publicly identified as Communists. With large sections of the public aroused over communism, use of a known Communist in a commercial movie would have reduced its audience and its money-making potential.

The blacklist damaged the careers, temporarily or permanently, of those it included. Some moved to the legitimate stage which had no mass audience and generally ignored the blacklist. Some found entirely new careers. Others moved to Europe to work in the foreign film industry where their Communist allegiance was not a liability. Some of the blacklisted screen writers secretly continued to work in the industry by using pseudonyms or having others act as "fronts" for their work. The blacklist lasted about ten years; by the late 1950s it was fading away. Its demise was announced by the success of the 1960 film *Spartacus*, based on a novel by the Communist writer Howard Fast and adapted for the screen by Dalton Trumbo, an ardent Stalinist who had been blacklisted.

HUAC's Hollywood forays and the sensitivity of the mass

entertainment industry to bad publicity spawned one of the morally questionable aspects of the era. With remarkable good luck in timing, in 1950, shortly before the Communist invasion of South Korea, three ex-FBI agents published *Red Channels*, listing 151 entertainers with Communist ties. The ex-agents started a business checking the names of entertainers against lists of Communists and fellow travelers they had compiled. Movie producers, radio and television networks, and sponsors of shows wishing to avoid controversy paid to make sure a possible star had not been an identifiable fan of Joseph Stalin. This type of "screening" activity could be abused. A few entertainers found themselves labeled as pro-Communist for having innocently or naively signed a few Popular Front petitions in the late 1930s. Fraught with even more conflict of interest, some of those in the screening business went into the business of clearing entertainers. For a fee, usually several hundred dollars, they would investigate and interview an entertainer with a record of signing on to Popular Front causes, then certify in a letter that the subject had been properly sensitized on the Communist issue. In a few cases the clearance business turned into a thinly disguised form of low-level extortion. Often to get clearance, the entertainer would have to make a statement of self-criticism of having been naive or foolish. John Garfield, a leading movie star and once a luminary of the Hollywood Popular Front, signaled his conformity to the new era by publishing "I Was a Sucker for the Left Hook" in a popular magazine of the era.

As was perhaps appropriate for an industry that thrives on "hype," HUAC's ventures into Hollywood produced intense publicity but little of substance. Congress never gave serious attention to censoring movies for political content, and Hollywood continued to produce movies as it had always done. Jack Warner and other Hollywood executives promised the House Un-American Activities Committee that they would make anti-Communist movies, and they did. Most of these, however, were simple low-budget spy thrillers that in the context of the cold war would have been produced anyway. The few movies that attempted to deal with domestic communism were not very successful and tended to use the established gangster movie genre with Communists playing the gangster role. Warner's anti-Communist film was *My Son John*, a 1952 production in which a mother turns in her Communist spy son; the son confesses but is then murdered by Communist agents. It was a box-office bust. Not even John Wayne in the leading role could save *Big Jim McLain*, a 1950 film glorifying HUAC, from scant audiences. Complex politics did not lend itself to the movie screen.

Of more substance than HUAC's ventures into Hollywood was the testimony it heard from Elizabeth Bentley. After graduating from Vassar in the mid-1930s, Bentley had joined the Communist party. Later she became the lover of Jacob Golos, a high CPUSA official involved in the party's underground, and became his courier to various covert contacts. In 1943 Golos died of a heart attack, and Bentley took over his rings of informants in Washington. But Soviet intelligence took direct control of her network and pushed her out of underground work. In August 1945, disillusioned, depressed by Golos's death, and fearing the FBI was closing in on her, Bentley turned herself in.

Bentley told HUAC she had been the link between Soviet intelligence and two large rings of Communist informants inside the government. One group was headed by Victor Perlo, a government economist at the War Production Board, and the other by Nathan Silvermaster, an economist with the Board of Economic Warfare. Bentley, however, had only her own testimony to back up her story; she had kept no documents or other evidence. Most of those named by Bentley refused to be questioned under oath about her story, invoking their Fifth Amendment right not to testify, and none confessed under questioning by the FBI. U.S. authorities had decoded Soviet cable messages that confirmed sections of Bentley's story but decided not to use the information in prosecutions because they did not wish to alert the Soviets to the success of American code-breaking.

One of the few named by Bentley who did testify was William Remington. He admitted meeting with Bentley but said he thought she was a journalist and that he was providing her with innocent information. He also denied under oath that he had been a participant in various Communist organizations. The government, however, had evidence other than Bentley's that Remington had been an active Communist, and he was convicted of perjury. Espionage played only a minor role in Remington's perjury case and offered no dramatic confirmation of Bentley's overall story of a major spying operation. Remington's trial was also confused by serious procedural irregularities (the foreman of the grand jury that first indicted Remington also collaborated with Bentley in publishing her autobiography), and his conviction was thrown out on appeal. The evidence of Remington's perjury was strong nonetheless; the government retried the case and convicted Remington a second time. He was jailed and was later murdered in prison in a fight with other inmates.

Also named by Bentley was Harry Dexter White, an influential Treasury Department official. Bentley testified that White was not a Communist but was a strong ally and supplied sensitive information to her spy ring. But she could not claim that she knew this from personal knowledge, because she did not deal with White directly but through Nathan Silvermaster. Her evidence was therefore indirect at best. White immediately responded to Bentley. He told HUAC that while he had known Silvermaster, he had no knowledge of any Soviet espionage and never had contact with any covert Communist group. Later, the former Soviet spy Whittaker Chambers produced a lengthy document in White's handwriting that cast much doubt on White's denials. But the case was not pursued because White died of a heart attack shortly after his testimony.

Reactions to Bentley's testimony followed patterns similar to those in the *Amerasia* case. Republicans depicted Bentley's testimony as more proof that the Democratic administration had harbored Soviet spies, either from incompetence or even from active collaboration by treacherous New Deal officials. The Truman administration assumed a defensive posture, pursued the Bentley case only when pushed by Congress, and was relieved when the FBI could not produce sufficient evidence to prosecute most of those named by Bentley. Anti-Communist liberals tended to believe Bentley, but they were uneasy about the vagueness of her testimony and her inability to produce much collabo-ration. Popular Front liberals simply dismissed her as too silly to be believed and ridiculed her at every turn.

Bentley's credibility was damaged because she had named scores of government employees as spies but only William Rem-ington, a minor figure, had gone to prison. Nor did it help that her autobiography, *Out of Bondage*, abounded in melodrama and scenes that read like pulp-magazine spy stories. The passage of time, however, has verified Bentley's testimony. World War II NKVD messages decoded by the U.S. government's secret Venona project but not released until 1995 confirmed that most of those named as Soviet spies by Bentley were just what she said. The messages verified Jacob Golos's role as an intermediary to various Soviet sources and showed Nathan Silvermaster, head of one of Bentley's networks, providing the NKVD with docu-ments on U.S. weapons production. Venona confirmed Bentley's claim that several OSS officials, including a high-ranking ad-viser to the head of the OSS, were Soviet spies. Venona also con-firmed Bentley's controversial claim that Lauchlin Currie, an aide to President Roosevelt, assisted Soviet intelligence. The de-coded messages showed Currie providing the Soviets with diplo-matic intelligence and warning them that the FBI had begun to suspect Silvermaster. Venona, along with documents found in newly opened Soviet archives about Victor Perlo and others Bentley had named as part of the Perlo group, showed that the often doubted Bentley was telling the truth.

When Elizabeth Bentley testified to the House Un-American Activities Committee in 1948, an additional witness was called to collaborate part of her story. That witness, Whittaker Chambers, produced testimony that quickly overshadowed hers. Chambers was fat, short, dressed in a disheveled manner, and spoke in a monotone. Despite his underwhelming appearance and delivery, the story he told was anything but dull. Chambers in the 1920s had been a bohemian poet who earned an income through trans-lation: *Bambi* was a Chambers translation from the German. He was also an open member of the Communist party and a radical journalist. In the early 1930s he dropped out of the open party and became a member of the Communist party's secret apparatus which he said was headed by J. Peters. For decades many historians refused to believe there was a CPUSA underground of the sort Chambers described, or that J. Peters had anything to do with it. Peters himself ridiculed the idea of there being any sort of Communist underground. After the collapse of the Soviet Union, however, documents found in the Soviet archives showed that the CPUSA's secret apparatus was just as Chambers described— and it was, as he said, headed by Peters. Chambers claimed he had been transferred from the American Communist underground to Soviet intelligence work in the mid-1930s but had quit in 1938. He attributed his defection to disillusionment with communism and fear that he was about to become a victim of Stalin's bloody purge of the Soviet intelligence apparatus. Chambers reentered journalism and by 1948 had become a senior editor for *Time* magazine.

Chambers testified that among his assignments with the CPUSA's underground was that of assisting secret Communists who worked for government agencies in Washington in the 1930s. He named several members of one group at the Agricultural Adjustment Administration in the mid-1930s. (There is no doubt this group existed because several people named by Chambers later confirmed its existence, though some gave benign accounts of its activities.) Some of those he named overlapped with names provided by Elizabeth Bentley.

But the most prominent name Chambers provided was one Bentley had not offered in her public testimony, that of Alger Hiss. Hiss was the archetype of the young New Dealer, an idealistic lawyer (Harvard Law School graduate, law clerk for the Supreme Court) who had left a prestigious law firm to work for the New Deal's economic reform agencies. Later he became a State Department official and accompanied President Roosevelt to the vital Yalta Conference with Stalin and Churchill in 1945. He was also a leading figure in the American delegation to the founding conference of the United Nations. By the time Chambers testified, Hiss had left the State Department and was director of the Carnegie Endowment for Peace, a prestigious private foundation.

Hiss immediately denounced Chambers's charge in a HUAC hearing, flatly denying he had ever been a Communist, had ever been a member of a Communist group at the Agricultural Adjustment Administration, had ever had any sympathy for communism, or had ever known Chambers. Hiss was considerably more impressive than Chambers. He was slim, handsome, well dressed, and spoke forcefully, confidently, and with dignity. The audience applauded Hiss's remarks, laughed at his jokes, and snickered derisively at those few HUAC members who dared to ask hostile questions. When the hearing ended, Representative John Rankin rushed up to shake Hiss's hand: Rankin, relying on his prejudice that most Communists were Jews, was ready to believe that Hiss, a stereotypical WASP, was innocent.

The press almost unanimously found Hiss's testimony credible. Numerous newspaper stories and editorials blasted the House Un-American Activities Committee for having brought malicious charges against an honest patriot and dedicated public servant. The Truman administration, which regarded HUAC as a partisan tool of the Republicans, was delighted at what appeared to be a HUAC gaff and confidently looked forward to using the backlash against the attack on Hiss as a reason to get HUAC dissolved. After Hiss's testimony, President Truman publicly dismissed the House Un-American Activities Committee as a Republican diversion to hide its poor congressional record. Hiss's testimony was sufficiently impressive and the press reaction so pro-Hiss that most members of HUAC, including its Republican leadership, were ready to drop the issue. Freshman Representative Richard Nixon, however, persuaded HUAC to continue the investigation.

Richard Nixon grew up in southern California. His family was Quaker, as were many residents of his home town of Whittier. His father was first a farmer, then an oil field roustabout, and finally the operator of a small grocery store and gasoline station. After graduating from a small Quaker college and finishing law school, Nixon worked briefly in the wartime Office of Price Administration and then entered the navy. After war service in the Pacific, he returned to his home town and in 1946 ran for Congress. His opponent was Representative Jerry Voorhis, a veteran Democrat who had won election in that district for five terms and was a nationally known and respected liberal spokesman. Nixon campaigned as a conservative and benefited from voters' fatigue with the New Deal, a fatigue aptly caught by the Republican 1946 slogan of "Had Enough?" Nixon also skillfully used the public's rising disquiet over Soviet expansion to paint Voorhis as soft on communism.

Voorhis was not a Communist sympathizer or Popular Front liberal. While he had gotten along with the Communist faction in the California Democratic party in the late 1930s and with the Communist-led California CIO, he had not been one of their close allies. When the Nazi-Soviet pact was signed, Popular Front liberals broke with Roosevelt, but Voorhis supported the president and wrote the Voorhis Anti-Propaganda Act strengthening the regulation of organizations linked to foreign nations. Voorhis intended the statute to hit both pro-Nazi and Communist organizations, and it forced the CPUSA officially to sever its links to the Communist International. But when Hitler's invasion of the Soviet Union moved American Communists to support Roosevelt's policies, Voorhis was once more willing to work with them. In 1944 he welcomed endorsement by the California CIO's Political Action Committee, a body dominated by Harry Bridges, a concealed Communist who headed the International Longshoremen's and Warehousemen's Union. It was Voorhis's bad luck that when he faced Nixon in 1946, the split between anti-Communist liberals and Popular Front liberals was only in its early stages. Had that split been more developed and Voorhis clearly on the anti-Communist side, Nixon would have had little opening. But as it was, Voorhis's 1944 endorsement by the Political Action Committee was still fresh, and the National Citizens Political Action Committee, a Communist-led spin-off of the CIO's Political Action Committee, had tentatively endorsed Voorhis in 1946. Nixon used the Political Action Committee issue to link Voorhis to communism, the leading role of semiconcealed Communists in the California CIO Political Action Committee being well known to California voters. Voorhis never developed a convincing response. To political activists it was clear that Voorhis was not in the Popular Front camp, but this was not obvious to ordinary voters.

Although Nixon's charges against Voorhis were unfair, they were also well within the raucous traditions of American electoral politics. The use of the Communist issue by Nixon and other Republicans in 1946 was, to cite but two examples, no better and no worse than that of Democrats in the early 1940s who depicted isolationist Republicans as pro-Nazi fifth columnists doing Hitler's work, or of Democrats in 1987 and 1988 who charged Republican presidents Reagan and Bush with entering into a treasonous conspiracy with the Ayatollah Khomeini of Iran.

Republicans won control of Congress in 1946, gaining fifty-six House and thirteen Senate seats. In view of the success of the Communist issue in the 1946 election, Republicans hoped to use their newly won control of the House Un-American Activities Committee to give the issue more attention as well as further harassing the Democrats and embarrassing the Truman administration in the run-up to the 1948 election. Republican leaders put Nixon on HUAC where they hoped his intelligence and sophistication would leaven a body that lacked both.

Nixon quickly made himself into one of the best-informed members of Congress on the issue of domestic communism. He held a series of lengthy meetings with Father John Cronin, one of the Catholic church's experts on American communism. It was from Cronin that Nixon first heard about Whittaker Chambers and Alger Hiss. Many of HUAC's members paid only perfunctory attention to the committee's witnesses, often asking abusive questions or making statements designed to win press attention rather than elicit information. Nixon, on the other hand, closely followed the testimony and carefully read the reports of HUAC's investigative staff.

It was the Hiss case that raised Nixon from the status of an ambitious but still obscure freshman congressman to a national figure. It was Nixon who suggested that Chambers be questioned by HUAC to provide collaboration for Elizabeth Bentley. And it was Nixon's questioning that elicited from Chambers that in 1939 he had gone to Adolf A. Berle, assistant secretary of state and a Roosevelt adviser, with his information about Alger Hiss and other concealed Communists in the government, and had told the same story to the FBI in 1943 and 1945—but little had happened. This testimony made the Democratic administration look casual about the problem of concealed Communists.

Hiss's persuasive rebuttal, however, pushed aside Chambers's testimony. Hiss looked and sounded like what he was: a highly respected, sophisticated, and socially connected member of the Washington establishment. Hiss's connections were bipartisan, with ties to Dean Acheson, a senior diplomat whose Democratic connections would soon make him Truman's secretary of state, and to John Foster Dulles, the likely secretary of state should the Republican Thomas E. Dewey win in 1948 (he actually was named to the post upon Eisenhower's election), who chaired the board of the Carnegie Endowment for Peace that Hiss directed.

HUAC's leadership, in a panic after Hiss's impressive showing, was ready to abandon the issue. But Nixon knew more of the background than they. From his briefing sessions with Father Cronin, Nixon knew that Chambers's testimony had some basis in fact. Nixon knew that Hiss, despite his untarnished public reputation, had been quietly eased out of the State Department in late 1946 into the Carnegie Endowment because Truman administration officials, alarmed by information turned up in FBI reports, feared he would become an embarrassment. Nixon also had a good ear for testimony and felt that on key issues Hiss had used language that sounded like a broad denial but came down to a denial only of a select point—a type of evasion.

Nixon prevailed, and HUAC recalled Chambers for executive (private) testimony. In this session Chambers provided a mass of details of a close relationship between himself and the Hiss family during the 1930s, including Hiss's bird-watching habits and

Hiss having given Chambers rent-free use of an apartment. The committee then called in Hiss. In testimony about his personal habits he confirmed many of the points Chambers had made. HUAC then arranged a confrontation between the two, and Hiss began to backtrack, stating he had known Chambers but under a different name (George Crosley) and only casually. He continued to deny any Communist connections.

HUAC also produced evidence that corroborated a multitude of details of Hiss's personal life that Chambers had discussed and which were difficult to reconcile with Chambers having been the casual acquaintance Hiss said he was. In renewed public hearings Hiss was on the defensive. While he stuck to his Crosley story, he was evasive and unable to explain some charges and circumstances. Press coverage began to shift from overwhelmingly pro-Hiss to a more neutral stance.

Hiss responded to his pounding by HUAC with a challenge to Chambers to repeat his claims outside the hearing room. Chambers's testimony to a congressional committee was protected from private suit. If Chambers repeated his charges outside a committee hearing, Hiss promised to sue him for slander and in court prove that Chambers had lied. Chambers then repeated his charges on the television program "Meet the Press." Hiss, after a delay of three weeks that caused consternation among his many supporters, then sued.

In preparation for the libel trial, Hiss's lawyers, confident there were none, demanded that Chambers produce any documents to support his charge that Hiss had been a Communist. Chambers, it turned out, did have documents, documents he hadn't told HUAC about. He was now legally obliged to provide them and, in any case, Hiss's suit had raised the stakes. Chambers needed to defend himself. The documents included four sheets of paper in Hiss's handwriting; sixty-five typewritten documents which were copies of confidential State Department material that had passed through Hiss's office in 1938; four sheets in the handwriting of Harry Dexter White, another government employee whom both Bentley and Chambers had linked to the CPUSA underground; two microfilm reels of confidential State

Department documents from 1938 (many with Hiss's initials and office stamp on them); and two microfilm reels of confidential Navy Department documents from 1938.

The Chambers documents did not show that Hiss was a secret member of the Communist party; they showed something much worse: Hiss had been a spy. Chambers explained that, as he had previously testified, he had begun his underground work for the Communist party as a link between the party and underground Communists in the government. Later, however, he said he, Hiss, and others were transferred by the American Communist party to the control of Soviet intelligence and became spies. Once in the State Department, Hiss had provided Chambers with a stream of government documents that Chambers microfilmed and passed on to a Soviet intelligence officer. Chambers testified that when he decided to break with Soviet intelligence in 1938, he had retained some material as a safeguard. Through intermediaries he informed the CPUSA and his Soviet intelligence contacts that he had compromising material hidden in the hands of a third party who would give it to the authorities if Chambers or his family were harmed.

The first reaction of the Justice Department was to consider an indictment against Chambers, not Hiss. Chambers had earlier testified under oath that he knew of no espionage, so the newly produced documents were proof that he had perjured himself. Indicting Chambers would serve the short-term political needs of the Truman administration. Chambers was a political embarrassment because he gave credence to Republican complaints about the negligence of the Roosevelt and Truman administrations toward the internal threat of Communist subversion. Indicting Chambers as a perjurer would also reduce his credibility. Of course, Chambers had only perjured himself if the documents were true, if Chambers was now telling the truth, and if Hiss had been a spy.

An indictment against Chambers might also allow the administration to keep many of his documents secret because of their potential use as evidence in a trial. Nixon and HUAC sought to head this off by making many of the documents public. When

HUAC's investigators went to Chambers's Maryland farm to pick up some of the documents, Chambers took them to a hollowed-out pumpkin where he had hidden them. According to Chambers, he had temporarily placed them there in case some of Hiss's partisans tried to steal them before HUAC got them. This weird hiding place also might have been a melodramatic device to add press attention to the event. Whatever the motivation, the press quickly dubbed the documents the "pumpkin papers."

In the glare of publicity, the Justice Department's contemplated action appeared absurd—the repentant spy was to be jailed but the unrepentant was to go free? Belatedly the Justice Department launched a grand jury inquiry to determine if Hiss or Chambers was right about Hiss's role in Soviet espionage. The investigation concluded with an indictment for perjury against Hiss. (The statute of limitation had expired for an espionage charge, but the charge of having lied under oath to the grand jury that he had ever passed documents to Chambers was a way of getting at the same offense. The perjury charge also included Hiss having lied about when he had known Chambers.) Hiss's first trial resulted in a hung jury, but most of the jurors had voted to convict, and the government retried the case. The second trial resulted in a conviction in January 1950. Hiss was imprisoned for three and a half years.

The evidence presented at Hiss's trial, and that which has surfaced since, was and is convincing. Numerous witnesses and documents confirmed that Chambers and Hiss were closely associated until 1938, in contradiction of Hiss's claim that his contact with Chambers was casual and did not extend beyond 1936. Vincent Reno and Julian Wadleigh, government employees whom Chambers had also named as members of his spy ring, confessed. Three photographers who worked for the ring confirmed that they had microfilmed documents for Chambers. In 1977 Nadya Ulanovsky, a Soviet intelligence agent, defected from the USSR and confirmed her role as a supervisor of Chambers's espionage activities in 1934. In 1992, after the collapse of the Soviet Union, documents found in Russian archives confirmed Chambers's testimony about the existence of an American Communist party underground operating in Washington in the 1930s and early 1940s and of J. Peters's role as its head. Most damning of all remain the pumpkin papers. Not only did these include documents in Hiss's own handwriting and microfilm of documents with Hiss's initials and office stamp on them, but expert analysis of the typewritten documents—sixty-five pages of confidential State Department material—showed conclusively that almost all had been typed on Hiss's own typewriter kept at his home.

Hiss continued to proclaim his innocence in prison and in 1995 still sought vindication. (Chambers died in 1961.) There remains to this day a vocal group of Hiss supporters who back his position, claiming that Chambers framed Hiss, either on his own or in conspiracy with the FBI. The theories developed by Hiss supporters have changed over the years. When it was first rumored that Chambers would testify, the Communist party launched a rumor campaign to discredit Chambers prior to his testimony; Washington reporters received unsolicited tips that Chambers was alcoholic, insane, and homosexual. From the beginning, Hiss and his supporters have put major weight on a psychological explanation for Chambers's claims. Most revolve around Chambers being a homosexual who developed a passion for Hiss during their casual acquaintance and who, when ignored, took revenge by framing Hiss for espionage. Chambers for his part admitted to having had homosexual experiences but denied interest in Hiss and claimed that in the mid-1930s he was exclusively heterosexual.

In another defense theory, Chambers is asserted to have been a Soviet spy who used his espionage apparatus to frame Hiss, an innocent patriot, by having Julian Wadleigh steal handwritten notes and other documents from Hiss's office. Later Hiss defense theories held that Chambers was chiefly the agent of an FBI conspiracy. Hiss defenders asserted that the FBI and J. Edgar Hoover framed Hiss in order to discredit the New Deal; this the FBI did by forging the pumpkin papers and blackmailing witnesses to perjure themselves by testifying against Hiss.

In late 1992 a new version of the Hiss defense surfaced. This was based on a claim by a prominent Russian historian that there were no documents in Soviet archives showing that Hiss or Chambers had any link to Soviet intelligence. The historian later withdrew his statement, saying he had not had access to the relevant archives. Hiss partisans, however, have ignored the retraction and hold that the original statement proves that the entire episode was a Chambers fantasy—not only was Hiss not a spy, but Chambers was not either. In this version Chambers was not only a frustrated homosexual but a mentally unbalanced pathological liar. Hiss supporters asserted that Chambers created a mythical nightmare of Soviet espionage into which he imagined Hiss. Chambers then won assent to his fantasy from the FBI, the Justice Department, and a jury because in the anti-Communist paranoia of 1950 even fantasies were believed. This latest Hiss defense simply wishes away the confessions of Wadleigh and Reno, the testimony of Chambers's photographers, and the evidence of the pumpkin papers. Although still contested by Hiss partisans, the weight of historical evidence is convincing that Chambers was a Communist and a Soviet spy who defected in 1938, and that in the 1930s Hiss was just what Chambers said he was: a secret Communist and a spy for the Soviet Union.

5

Varieties of Anticommunism

ANTICOMMUNISM FROM the late 1940s to the late 1950s was unusually powerful because virtually every anti-Communist constituency was mobilized. Without an appreciation of the full variety of this mobilization, an understanding of the anti-Communist era is only partial. We have already seen how the disparity between Roosevelt's promised democratic war aims and the reality of Soviet rule in Eastern Europe aroused anti-Communist sentiment among ethnic groups and, more generally, liberal adherents to those war aims. The onset of the cold war in the late 1940s provided a framework for the mobilization of additional anti-Communist constituencies.

Practicing Christians quickly recognized communism as a deadly enemy. After the Soviets came to power in 1917, Lenin closed most churches and in 1922 ordered an attack on believers in which Soviet security police executed between fourteen thousand and twenty thousand priests, monks, nuns, and active laymen. Religiously motivated anticommunism had its principal constituencies at opposite ends of the American religious spectrum: evangelical Protestants and Roman Catholics.

Until after World War II, most American evangelicals were hostile to communism but did not regard it as a unique or especially powerful threat. Evangelical Christians tended to see communism simply as an extreme and violent strain of a more general menace to Christianity: the threat of secular and atheistic modernism. In the 1920s Christians who held to biblical inerrancy and a literal reading of Genesis, for example, regarded the increasing acceptance and teaching of Darwinian evolution as a far more immediate concern than a distant Soviet communism. Similarly, most evangelical preachers spent more time deploring loose sexual mores, immodest dress, erotic popular music, materialism, and self-indulgent individualism than they did communism.

Most evangelical denominations also adhered to a congregational form of church governance that rejected central control and leadership. Consequently leadership was diffuse and localized. While individual evangelical preachers in the 1920s and 1930s occasionally emphasized the inherent hostility between Christianity and communism, such occurrences were usually isolated and brief. In general, evangelical Christianity contributed passively to the general public suspicion of communism. Not until the end of World War II and the emergence of the Soviet Union as a world power viewed as threatening the United States did anticommunism become a major topic of most evangelical preachers.

After World War II, however, Protestant evangelical Christians became a significant source of active anti-Communist agitation. Their religious and their patriotic beliefs blended: a threat to one was perceived as a threat to the other. The cold war division of the world between the Western alliance led by the United States and the Communist bloc under the suzerainty of the Soviet Union; the irredeemably hostile nature of the Communist threat to the values held by evangelical Christians; and the apocalyptic nature of the contest, with its menace of nuclear catastrophe, resonated to evangelicals steeped in the Christian millenarian tradition. Indeed, so grim were the early years of the cold war, following as they did the horrors of World War II, and so widespread were the expectations of a nuclear war, that to a segment of evangelicals the prophecies of the Book of Revelation seemed to be fulfilled: Stalin appeared to be the Antichrist, and Armageddon, when the last battle between good and evil would be joined before the Day of Judgment, was drawing nigh. In the pulpits of thousands of evangelical churches, preachers shifted from describing communism as only one of the many sins of modern times to being a chief evil of the era.

A major supplier of anti-Communist information to fundamentalist preachers was the Church League of America. This organization had its origins among fundamentalists who were deeply hostile to theological modernism and to liberal and left-wing politics. It was not a mass-membership organization but a resource and propaganda body that produced brochures, studies, and pamphlets and maintained extensive cross-indexed files on the links between liberal Christian pastors and left-wing political activity. Some of its pamphlets presented theological modernism as part of a Communist plot and suggested that denominations in which modernism was predominant, such as the Methodists, Episcopalians, and Presbyterians, had been infiltrated by Communists who pretended to be Christians.

Several small, distinctly evangelical organizations also emerged, such as the Christian Anti-Communist Crusade. This California-based group was the vehicle of Fred Schwarz, an Australian immigrant, lay Baptist preacher, and medical doctor. His book, *You Can Trust the Communists (To Do Exactly as They Say)*, was a strident, simplified exposition of Marxism-Leninism with quotes from leading Communists designed to show that communism was anti-Christian, aggressive, and bent on world domination. Schwarz presented his message in lectures, radio and TV programs, and "crusades" modeled after Protestant revivals. His Christian Anti-Communist Crusade was particularly attractive to fundamentalist Christians with a Republican background. Similar, but with an appeal to evangelical Christians with a history of voting Democratic, was the Oklahoma-based "Christian Crusade" of evangelist Billy James Hargis.

The Schwarz and Hargis organizations never attracted the support of more than a small fraction of evangelical Christians. Rather than expressing itself in specifically Christian anti-Communist organizations, Protestant evangelical anticommunism motivated believers to join a variety of largely secular anti-Communist bodies and to direct their votes to political candidates who articulated an anti-Communist stance.

Although the United States had originated as a largely Protestant nation, by the middle of the twentieth century heavy immigration and large families had made Roman Catholics, while still a minority of Americans, the largest single religious community in the nation. Communism and the Roman Catholic church perceived each other as deadly enemies at an early date. Like evangelical Protestants, the Roman Catholic church tended to see communism not as a unique threat but as a particularly violent and malevolent variety of the general evil of atheistic modernism. But because of its worldwide scope and its extensive membership in Central and Eastern Europe, the Roman church saw communism as a more direct threat much earlier than did American Protestants with their more parochial institutional outlook. American Catholic intellectuals also developed in the 1930s a complex analysis of Soviet communism, an interpretation that in its sophistication was rivaled only by those developed by left anti-Communists. Father Edmund A. Walsh, vice-president of Georgetown University and a leading scholar of Soviet affairs, served as the unofficial spokesman for the American Roman Catholic church on Soviet affairs. In a number of books and essays he analyzed the convergence of Marxism-Leninism's aspiration for universal rule with the imperial ambitions and traditions of Russian nationalism. In the 1930s and early 1940s Walsh's views were a decidedly minority voice, but when the cold war developed in the late 1940s, the influence of his interpretation soared as events vindicated his analysis. By that time as well, the students he had taught were coming into positions of influence in all walks of American life.

The most decisive event in arousing Roman Catholic anticommunism was the Spanish Civil War. Both sides in the conflict committed massive atrocities against civilians, but the Catholic church became one of the main targets of the left-wing revolutionary violence that provided the occasion for Francisco Franco's revolt against the Spanish Republic in 1936. During the civil war that followed, more than five thousand churches were destroyed and between six thousand and seven thousand priests, monks, and nuns were murdered.

The tales from Spain of murder, rape, and torture directed at the church horrified the American Catholic faithful. Although the most active and violent force in the antireligious terror in Spain were anarcho-syndicalists, Catholics tended to place major blame on the Communists because of their high visibility in the Spanish Republican government. To most Catholic clergy and faithful, the issue of Spain was clear: Franco's forces, whatever their flaws, were fighting to maintain a Christian civilization while the Republic was atheistic, Communist, and condoned the murder of priests and the rape of nuns. The debate within the United States over government policy toward the Spanish Civil War was intense, and American Communists were among the loudest voices in support of the Spanish Republic. This caused part of Catholic distress over Spain to be directed against American Communists as well as against Spanish Communists and the Soviet Union. And since most American liberals supported the Republic—and were supportive of the Republic's anticlerical policies and indifferent to the anti-Catholic terror—Catholic hostility extended as well to Popular Front liberals.

After World War II, communism emerged as the single most powerful institutional opponent of Roman Catholicism. Stalin's takeover of Eastern Europe brought with it persecution of Catholics in Poland, Czechoslovakia, and Hungary, homelands of large Catholic populations. A murderous persecution of Catholics unleashed by the Communist victory in China nearly extinguished the Chinese church. Added to these losses were the threats of Communist takeovers in France and Italy, also nations with large Catholic populations. In the face of this challenge, devout Catholics throughout the world came to regard active anticommunism as a requirement of their faith. American bishops, anticipating a postwar struggle with communism, in early 1945 commissioned a special study of the problem by Father John Cronin, a Maryknoll priest and teacher. Cronin had become acquainted with communism in the early 1940s when he assisted

Catholic workers in Local 43 of the CIO's Industrial Union of Marine and Shipbuilding Workers, at the Bethlehem Fairfield shipyard in Baltimore. Cronin quickly realized that the Baltimore CIO's chief organizer and many of his associates were secret Communists and supported a pro-Communist faction inside Local 43. For several years a Communist-dominated faction and a Cronin-supported group fought for control of the local. Although he was ultimately defeated, Father Cronin received a practical lesson in the nature of American communism.

In late 1944 Cronin's church superiors realized that his experience and his considerable skills as a teacher and Catholic analyst of social problems fitted him for the task of outlining an anti-Communist strategy for the American church. Cronin's study was particularly well informed because he had established a close relationship with William Sullivan, an FBI agent who took a strong interest in Communist matters. Sullivan privately leaked to Cronin information the FBI had developed about Communist infiltration of various government agencies during the 1930s and early 1940s, evidence that the Roosevelt and Truman administrations had not energetically pursued. Cronin's 1945 report even noted the evidence pointing to secret Communist sympathies by Alger Hiss, the prominent and highly regarded American diplomat—three years before Whittaker Chambers accused Hiss of having been a secret Communist and a Soviet spy.

Anticommunism in the postwar period also fitted the particular institutional needs of the American church. While religious tolerance had generally prevailed in America, Protestant attitudes had continued to dominate American culture until well into the twentieth century. Catholicism had been looked down upon as the religion of ill-assimilated immigrants: the Irish in the nineteenth century and Slavs in the twentieth. At several points in American history, powerful anti-Catholic movements had arisen which portrayed Catholics as either entirely un-American or incapable of assimilation into American nationalism. The 1930s had seen a large measure of acceptance of Catholicism by the inclusion of Catholic ethnic constituencies in the New Deal coalition. World War II provided another push as government war propaganda stressed that Americans of all faiths and creeds were fighting together to win the war for democracy. When Soviet communism emerged as America's chief foreign rival in the late 1940s, Catholic anticommunism echoed American cold war patriotism. American Catholics, in expressing anticommunism, simultaneously affirmed both their Catholicism and their Americanism. In this sense, anticommunism served to complete the Americanization of the Roman Catholic church in the United States.

In the late 1940s and 1950s, opposition to communism became a regular item on the Catholic agenda. The American church possessed formidable institutional power, with more than fifty thousand priests, nuns, monks, and other religious who ministered to the spiritual needs of tens of millions. Articles about the arrests of priests, the closing of convents, and the confiscation of church property by the Communist regimes of Eastern Europe appeared regularly in parish and diocesan newspapers throughout the United States. It was a rare pastor who did not include a homily or two about the Communist threat to the Catholic faith as part of the yearly cycle of sermons that accompanied the Mass. Nor could any of the hundreds of thousands of students attending parochial schools miss lectures and classes about the Communist threat. The Knights of Columbus, a male Catholic fraternal order with more than a million members, educated its own followers about the threat of communism to the faith. Often Knights of Columbus chapters, of which there were more than five thousand, sponsored anti-Communist activities at the local level, as did the Catholic war veterans association.

One of the most influential Catholic voices was that of Fulton J. Sheen. A powerful and eloquent orator, as a young priest in the 1930s Sheen developed a wide audience through a highly popular radio program, "The Catholic Hour." Father Sheen devoted his sermons chiefly to explaining Catholic theology. But a number of his talks also applied Catholic doctrine to the problems of the day, and anticommunism was a regular, though not central, feature of his program. American Communists were rarely a particular target of Sheen's oratory, but few of his listeners distinguished between Soviet and American Communists. After television developed, Sheen made an almost effortless transfer to the new medium, and his television program "Life Is Worth Living" was so popular that in 1952 Sheen, by this time an auxiliary bishop, won an Emmy as the year's outstanding television personality. By 1954 his television show was carried by 170 stations and reached an audience of 25 million.

Catholic workers had always been heavily represented in the ranks of the American Federation of Labor (AFL), and their presence served to reaffirm the union's steadfast hostility to communism. The most dynamic labor development in the 1930s, however, was the organization of unskilled and semiskilled production workers by the CIO. A very large portion of these workers were Catholics, particularly those of Central and Eastern European origin. As labor turmoil developed in the 1930s, Catholic activists became involved. Most Catholic labor activists were inspired by two papal encyclicals, *Rerum Novarum* (1891) and *Quadragesimo Anno* (1931), that sought to apply Catholic social morality to the economic problems of modern industrial capitalism. Both encyclicals strongly condemned Marxism and communism as inherently inimical to Catholicism, but they were also highly critical of unrestrained capitalism and called for public intervention in the economy to ensure basic welfare. Both encyclicals gave Catholic sanction to the right of workers to organize themselves and bargain with employers to achieve fair wages and treatment that accorded with the dignity of the human soul.

The encyclicals inspired a number of Catholic campaigns aimed at improving the lot of workers and creating public and private welfare institutions. One such campaign was the Catholic Worker Movement that established settlement houses and soup kitchens in some of the most economically depressed urban areas of the United States. In 1937 several Catholic Worker Movement activists led by Martin Wersing, an organizer for the CIO's Utility Workers Union, founded the Association of Catholic Trade Unionists (ACTU). ACTU was a lay-led movement, though Catholic clergy served as chaplains for ACTU chapters and some individual priests had considerable influence within it. It was not a mass-membership organization aimed at enlisting Catholic workers. ACTU concentrated on creating a cadre of Catholic union militants imbued with ACTU's philosophy, who would provide leadership and direction for the broad mass of Catholic workers within existing labor unions.

Most of ACTU's work was with the CIO. In a number of important CIO organizing strikes in the late 1930s, employers sought to discredit the unions by charging that the CIO was Communist controlled, a potentially damaging charge with Catholic workers. ACTU intervened in these cases with defenses of the CIO and reassured Catholic workers that they could join the union in good conscience. One of the most influential priests in ACTU was Father Charles Owen Rice of Pittsburgh. When Martin Carmody, head of the powerful Catholic Knights of Columbus, accused the CIO of being Communist dominated, Rice responded with a vigorous defense of the CIO. When John Frey, a prominent AFL leader, accused John Brophy, one of the CIO's leading officials, of links to the Communist party, Father Rice exonerated Brophy (a practicing Catholic) and forced Frey to retreat. When CIO unions needed a story in a local paper about the compatibility of Catholicism with unionism, Father Rice would supply it. When CIO strikers wanted Catholic placards on the picket line, Father Rice and ACTU were there.

While the Association of Catholic Trade Unionists defended the CIO against charges that it was Communist controlled, it had no sympathy for communism. ACTU regarded communism as the deadly enemy of Christianity and worked against Communists within the CIO as vigorously as it defended the union. In every union that contained both Communists and ACTU activists, they clashed. One of the chief battlegrounds was the United Electrical Workers, the CIO's third-largest union. ACTU was allied with James Carey, one of the union's founders and its first president. A Communist-led faction, however, controlled the union's largest locals, and in 1940 it removed Carey as head of the union. Thereafter Carey headed a large but minority anti-Communist faction in the union that relied on ACTU as its chief base.

Until the end of World War II, CIO anti-Communists were mostly frustrated in their assaults on the CIO's Communist-led faction. Part of this was due to the superior discipline of the Communists in the CIO's Popular Front wing. In contrast, the CIO's anti-Communist faction was a loose coalition of ACTU, Socialists, Trotskyists, and a variety of other types of anti-Communists.

The chief source of CIO anti-Communist frustration, however, was with the CIO's dominant centrist faction led by Philip Murray. Murray, himself a devout Catholic, accepted the teachings of *Rerum Novarum* and *Quadragesimo Anno* and was utterly opposed to communism. When Murray's own union, the United Steelworkers of America, was organized in the late 1930s, it utilized a large number of Communist organizers. But as soon as the union was on its feet, Murray quietly fired Communists from his staff and crushed attempts to form a Communist-led left caucus in the union. He was also on friendly terms with the Association of Catholic Trade Unionists, and it was Murray's support that allowed James Carey to retain his important post as the CIO's secretary-treasurer even after he lost the presidency of the United Electrical Workers. Yet after Murray became president of the CIO in 1941, he rejected ACTU's call for a more aggressive stand against the CIO's Communists, not wishing to disrupt the CIO's internal stability. Until Murray changed his mind, ACTU and the CIO's anti-Communists were unable to mount a broad attack on the CIO's Communists.

Until the late 1940s, CIO Communists won more battles than they lost with the Association of Catholic Trade Unionists, but even in winning they paid a price. ACTU's presence in a union almost always put Communists in a defensive mode. When an anti-Communist faction gathered about a local's ACTU-trained activists, Communists reduced their prominence in the local's leadership in order to present a smaller target for anti-Communist attack. Communist-led unions with an active ACTU minority often withheld support for Communist-linked political activity because such activity offered ACTU an opportunity to charge Communist domination of the union.

Communist unionists, however, were always hostages to the political stance of the CPUSA. After World War II, American Communists, always loyal to Moscow, shifted their stance from one of support for established liberal leaders to one of harsh opposition to the policies of President Truman. When Communists decided to support the Progressive party candidacy of Henry Wallace in 1948, they burned their bridges with Philip Murray and the centrist faction of the CIO.

Once Murray and his centrist faction became actively anti-Communist, ACTU's room to maneuver greatly expanded. Only in a few unions, and then usually only in a few locals, did ACTU play a direct organizational role by sponsoring an anti-Communist caucus. More important, as CIO leaders looked for reliable unionists to replace those linked to the Communist party, ACTU provided a pool of activists already trained in the basics of unionism and prepared to take on the task of expelling Communists from the labor movement. Hundreds of workers who had passed through ACTU's training sessions in parliamentary procedure, organizing, labor law, bookkeeping, and, of course, Catholic social philosophy and anticommunism, became officials of union locals.

Before World War I the Socialist Party of America appeared to be on the brink of becoming a political force. Two factors destroyed its prospects. First, the Socialists strongly opposed America's entry into the war, causing a sizable prowar faction to leave the party. In the atmosphere of aroused patriotism and war mobilization, antiwar Socialist leaders and party locals were also subjected to prosecution and harassment. Second, the Bolshevik revolution split the party. Moderate Socialists who led the party rejected violent revolution and the Bolshevik doctrine of party dictatorship as appropriate for American Socialists. Fearing the growing power of the party's pro-Bolshevik faction, in 1919 the Socialist party leadership expelled its entire left wing which, in the initial infatuation with the Bolshevik revolution, constituted nearly two-thirds of the party's membership. The expelled group took with it many of the party's most aggressive and militant leaders and went on to found the American Communist party in 1919. Nonetheless, the Socialist party retained a sizable membership in New York City and a few other enclaves such as Milwaukee that was sufficient to keep the party alive.

In their continued rivalry with the Communist party, Socialists developed a thorough critique of communism from a left perspective. Principally, Socialists concentrated their attack on communism on the issue of democracy. The Socialist party held that socialism embodied democracy in every sphere of life—economic, political, social, and cultural. They rejected Lenin's variation of Marxism which held that the vanguard of committed Marxists, because they understood the laws of history, had the right to impose a socialist state by coercion. Socialists rejected communism on the grounds that although the Soviet Union had adopted overt forms of economic democracy by abolishing capitalism, its imposition of Communist party dictatorship in all other spheres of life resulted in a tyranny that was essentially nonsocialist. The Socialist ideological critique of communism from a left perspective hit communism on a vulnerable flank and placed a seed of doubt in the minds of many young radicals of the 1930s. It would later grow into a vigorous anticommunism under changed historical circumstances.

In addition to this theoretical critique, Socialists acted as conduits for information about the actual workings of the Soviet state and of the activities of Communists around the world. American Socialists had strong ties to the Mensheviks, those Russian socialists who rejected the doctrines of Lenin's Bolshevik faction. Mensheviks provided American Socialists with information about the extreme brutality of the "Red Terror" that the Bolsheviks used to exterminate their opponents during the Russian civil war. They also provided American Socialists with information about the Soviet suppression of dissent, the subordination of labor unions to the Communist party, and the replacement of the rule of law by the Communist party's administrative fiat. Socialists helped a number of exiled Mensheviks to reach the United States; in the 1940s these exiles were among the first to publish in English reliable accounts of the creation of the Soviet political police, the existence of the Gulag system of forced-labor camps, and the extensive Soviet system of foreign espionage and political subversion. Socialists played important roles in several labor and political struggles over communism. The anti-Communist wing of the International Ladies Garment Workers Union (ILGWU), largely led by Socialists, fought off a Communist attempt to control the national ILGWU leadership and eventually dislodged the Communists from their leading position in the large New York City locals. Similarly, Socialists in the Amalgamated Clothing Workers of America were key to blocking a determined Communist attempt to control that union. In 1936 Socialist leaders of the ILGWU and the Amalgamated Clothing Workers organized the American Labor party (ALP) as a vehicle for organizing liberal and left-of-center New York voters behind the Roosevelt New Deal. (The New York Democratic party, then dominated by the Tammany Hall political machine, was unenthusiastic about the New Deal and tainted by its history of corruption.) The American Labor party won sufficient votes to act as the balance of power between Republican and Democratic parties in the state. After the Communist party adopted its Popular Front stance and aligned itself with the New Deal, Communists moved into the ALP and attempted to take control of the newly influential organization. Socialists in the party fiercely resisted the Communist drive to make the ALP into a Popular Front organization by exposing Communists who hid their political stance and by publicizing the tactics of secret Communist-led caucuses in local ALP units.

The Nazi-Soviet pact was a major setback for Communists in the American Labor party who had championed antifascism and were now forced on the defensive by Stalin's alliance with Hitler. Further, a substantial portion of the American Labor party's voting constituency was Jewish, and many reacted to the Nazi-Soviet pact by shifting their support to the ALP's Socialist-led anti-Communist wing. After Hitler attacked the USSR in 1941, however, the ALP's Popular Front faction was able to regain the ground it had lost. In 1943 Communists formed an alliance with

Sidney Hillman, head of the Amalgamated Clothing Workers, by backing his plans to shift the ALP from its balance-of-power role between the two major parties to one of acting as a liberal-left adjunct to the Democratic party. This alliance was tied to Hillman's plans to ally the CIO's Political Action Committee to the Democratic party and Roosevelt's 1944 reelection campaign. Hillman's entry into a Popular Front alliance with the Communists infuriated many of the American Labor party's Socialists as well as David Dubinsky, head of the ILGWU. Dubinsky, the ILGWU, most of the American Labor party's Socialists, and other ALP anti-Communists walked out and formed the rival Liberal party. The Liberal party articulated an emphatic anti-Communist liberalism in contrast to the ALP's newly adopted Popular Front stance. The 1943 split and the ensuing struggle between the ALP and the Liberal party for control of the independent liberal-left vote in New York City presaged the conflict that would engulf liberals nationwide after World War II.

Socialists also provided activists for the anti-Communist wing of the CIO. When John L. Lewis founded the CIO and set out to organize the mass-production industries, he took in a number of Socialist organizers as well as Communist militants. These CIO Socialists were deeply suspicious of the Communists, spread the Socialist critique of communism within the CIO, and supported the CIO's anti-Communist faction. One of the most influential CIO Socialists was Adolph Germer. A tough and able organizer, Germer was Lewis's favorite troubleshooter when the CIO faced a particularly difficult or confused situation. Germer had served for many years as the Socialist party's national executive secretary and was fiercely anti-Communist. He tipped the balance to CIO anti-Communists in several angry fights with the CIO's Popular Front faction, such as in the nearly evenly split International Woodworkers of America in the Pacific Northwest.

Although the Socialist party continued to shrink in the decades after World War II (it changed its name to Social Democrats, USA in 1972), it kept on producing left anti-Communists who occupied key positions in the political action and foreign affairs arms of the American labor movement. For example, in the

1950s and 1960s the U.S. government, through the Central Intelligence Agency, covertly subsidized foreign prodemocratic and anti-Communist labor and political organizations in an effort to offset secret Soviet funding of Communist and pro-Soviet organizations. In the 1970s much of this activity was exposed, to the embarrassment of Washington and those who had been secretly subsidized. While covert funding of foreign organizations by the CIA came to be regarded as either improper or counterproductive, the U.S. government still felt a need to assist democratic movements that were in conflict with Soviet-subsidized opponents. Consequently in 1983 Congress established the National Endowment for Democracy, a publicly funded, quasi-private agency that openly provided training, advice, money, and supplies to democratic movements around the world. It first head was Carl Gershman, a former national secretary of Social Democrats, USA. Under Gershman, the National Endowment for Democracy assisted the Solidarity movement in Poland in its final push to overthrow the Communist regime there as well as other democratic movements that swept Communists out of power across Central Europe.

Another group of left anti-Communists had its origins in the Trotskyist splinter from the Communist movement. Leon Trotsky was second only to Lenin as a founder of Soviet communism, but after Lenin's death, he was outmaneuvered by Stalin in the struggle for succession. Trotsky's supporters were expelled from the Communist party; later in the 1930s Stalin had most Soviet Trotskyists executed. Trotsky himself was exiled from the USSR in 1929 and murdered by a Soviet assassin in Mexico in 1940.

The international Trotskyist movement was never a serious rival to the mainline Communist movement. Although it attracted talented individuals, its membership was never more than a fraction of that of the Communists, and it lacked the generous Soviet subsidies that sustained the pro-Soviet Communist parties. The small Trotskyist organizations were constantly harassed and disrupted, sometimes violently, by Soviet intelligence agents. Trotsky, however, was a talented writer, and his intellectual influence was much broader than his organization. Although Communist parties around the world engaged in an energetic campaign to rewrite history, Stalin failed to destroy Trotsky's reputation among radicals as one of the chief heroes of the Bolshevik revolution. His denunciation of Stalinist communism validated many of the charges of more conservative anti-Communists.

In the United States the Communist party's turn to the Popular Front in the mid-1930s caused it to drop its frontal assaults on bourgeois culture, such as avant-garde artistic forms and "proletarian" literature. Instead Communists embraced traditional art forms and conventional aesthetics, seeking simply to imbue them with politically correct content. A few radical intellectuals, who had been attracted by the party's revolutionary fervor and its staunch hostility to bourgeois culture, were disappointed by its bows to respectability and the ersatz "folkish" Americanism of the Popular Front. Trotskyism offered an alternative. Not only was Trotsky's combination of radical cultural criticism and revolutionary politics attractive, but the growing Stalinist attack on Trotsky culminating in the Moscow Purge Trials energized some American radicals and liberals to his defense. Trotskyism also gained support among intellectuals. Philip Rahv and William Phillips, editors of the *Partisan Review*, a lively literary journal that had once been aligned with the CPUSA, joined with writers James Farrell, Mary McCarthy, and Dwight Macdonald to form the core of a literary-intellectual opposition to the Communist party that for a time aligned itself with Trotskyism. Other intellectuals supported an inquiry organized by the prestigious liberal philosopher John Dewey into Stalin's charges that Trotsky had been betraying bolshevism since 1917 in league with various foreign intelligence services—an investigation which concluded that the Soviet Union's evidence was fraudulent.

The intellectual war of words grew heated as the 1930s drew to a close. The scandalous conduct of the Moscow Trials, where veteran Bolsheviks were forced to confess to absurd "counterrevolutionary" plots, promoted the formation of the Committee for Cultural Freedom that condemned totalitarianism of both the

right (Nazism and fascism) and the left (Soviet communism). Its manifesto was signed by 140 prominent intellectuals, led by John Dewey. The debate among intellectuals over the nature of the Soviet regime directly involved only a few hundred persons, and only a few of those had any political influence. John Dewey and the grouping of radical and liberal anti-Stalinist intellectuals were also a minority in the larger intellectual community. That community remained predominantly oriented to a Popular Front liberalism which took a benign view of Stalin and his work. Even so, the Committee for Cultural Freedom was an important development as it gave a vital measure of intellectual respectability to anticommunism and sketched out a coherent left anti-Communist position that, when anticommunism became a necessary attribute for any viable political position, would enable liberals and radicals to take a stance that upheld their left-wing views while freeing them of a totalitarian taint.

Another Communist splinter group led by Jay Lovestone also made major contributions to the anti-Communist cause. Lovestone had joined the Socialist party while in high school and was a delegate at the founding of the American Communist party in 1919. By 1921 he was a full-time functionary for the party. Lovestone had considerable intellectual talent and a knack for ruthless factionalism. By 1927, at the age of just twenty-nine, he and his followers had established their leadership over the faction-ridden American Communist movement.

Lovestone's ascendancy was due in part to his close ties to Nikolai Bukharin, a leading Bolshevik who headed the Communist International. After Bukharin, like Trotsky, lost out to Stalin in the contest to succeed Lenin, Lovestone and his followers renounced Bukharin. But Stalin nonetheless deposed Lovestone from the leadership of the American party. Lovestone and his chief lieutenants, Benjamin Gitlow and Bertram Wolfe, were expelled from the Communist party. For a few years thereafter Lovestone still considered himself a Communist; he and those few who had followed him out of the CPUSA called themselves the Communist Party (Majority Group), later renamed Communist Party (Opposition), and even continued to assist Soviet intelligence officers. Such loyalty to the Soviet Union, however, failed to win Lovestone readmission to the Communist movement. He became altogether alienated from the Communist enterprise when Stalin launched his murderous purges in the mid-1930s and executed Bukharin for treason after a show trial at which the veteran Bolshevik confessed to crimes he had never committed. In 1939 the Lovestone group abandoned Marxism-Leninism altogether and adopted a democratic socialist stance. The group also supported U.S. aid to those fighting Hitler, this at a time when those sympathetic to the Communist party were required by the Nazi-Soviet pact to oppose U.S. aid to the anti-Nazi belligerents. In 1941 Lovestone dissolved his group as a political body and devoted his time entirely to union work.

As Lovestone became increasingly hostile to Stalin, he and his small band of followers made themselves into a painful burr in the side of the Communist movement. Alarmed by the progress of Communist organizers in the newly organized CIO, Lovestone devoted his efforts to assisting anti-Communist labor activists. He unsuccessfully aided United Auto Worker president Homer Martin's attempt to defeat a powerful coalition of Communists, Socialists, and other radicals who opposed Martin's leadership. When the anti-Martin alliance won, Martin took a small fraction of the auto workers union into the AFL.

Lovestone's followers had better success in the ILGWU. A Lovestoneite leader, Charles Zimmerman, became a powerful figure in the union and worked closely with Socialists who led the union's dominant anti-Communist faction. ILGWU leader David Dubinsky recognized that Lovestone's intimate knowledge of the Communist movement both in the United States and abroad, and the ruthless factional skills he had honed as a Communist leader, would serve him well as an anti-Communist militant, and he helped Lovestone to become head of the Free Trade Union Committee. Initially the Committee aided European unionists and socialists to escape Nazi-occupied Europe. The Committee's goal was both short-term humanitarian assistance to refugees and long-range preservation of labor and socialist leaders who after the liberation of Europe could reconstruct a free union movement and a democratic socialist political movement.

After World War II the AFL threw its support behind the Free Trade Union Committee when it realized that in the political chaos and economic dislocation of liberation, the Communist parties of Western Europe, reinforced by Soviet money and the looming threat of the Soviet army, might greatly expand their influence over the union movement. Even before the Truman administration shifted to a cold war stance of resisting Soviet influence in Western Europe, the AFL embarked on a program of supporting non-Communist unionists and their socialist allies in a fierce struggle with European Communists and Communist-aligned unionists for control of working-class institutions and political bodies in Italy, France, Belgium, Greece, the Netherlands, West Germany, and Norway.

Lovestone argued, and the AFL agreed, that the United States could not rely on traditionally anti-Communist right-wing forces in Europe to hold back Soviet influence because the economic dislocation of the war had greatly enhanced the appeal of the left and because some on the right were tainted with Nazism. The key to halting Communist expansion, Lovestone said, was the creation of viable anti-Communist or at least non-Communist labor movements and of anti-Communist socialist parties in Western Europe. Lovestone directed the AFL's anti-Communist foreign campaign. He dispatched organizers to Europe largely drawn either from his old following or from anti-Communist American Socialists. Most were veterans of the struggle against Communists in the American labor movement. Lovestone and his organizers provided advice, money, and supplies to sympathetic European unionists.

When the Truman administration shifted to a cold war stance in 1947–1948, it largely accepted Lovestone's view that the left, not the right, was the battleground on which to win the ideological cold war in Western Europe. Washington created a corps of labor attachés at American embassies which operated in much the same way as Lovestone's organizers and often worked closely with them. The U.S. government also provided direct and indirect financial support for the Free Trade Union Committee's work, and the Central Intelligence Agency's covert-action arm provided secret subsidies for those labor and left or center-left political bodies that had the approval of Lovestone and the AFL.

Lovestone's strategy won a significant measure of success. In Belgium, the Netherlands, West Germany, and Norway the labor movements that developed after World War II were largely non-Communist, and the predominant left-of-center political parties were democratic socialists hostile to communism. In Italy and France, Communists won control of the largest union federations, but AFL-backed socialist or Catholic trade unionists won control of a sufficient number of unions to weaken seriously the power of the Communist-led union federations. In France the unions of the Lovestone-backed Force Ouvrière labor federation were key to breaking a general strike organized by Communist-led unions that threatened to plunge the nation into chaos and bring France's large Communist party to power.

After the AFL and the CIO merged in 1955, Lovestone became director of the AFL-CIO's International Department and expanded his foreign operations. Again working in tandem with the Eisenhower administration's cold war policies, the AFL-CIO blunted the drive by Communists to take control of labor movements in Africa, Asia, and South America. After Lovestone's retirement his policies were continued by his successor, Irving Brown, a veteran Lovestone supporter who had directed the AFL's operations in Europe.

Brown's successor, Tom Kahn, was two generations younger than Lovestone but was the lineal descendant of another Communist schism of the late 1920s. Kahn entered left politics in the 1960s by way of a group headed by Max Shachtman, once a CPUSA activist and one of the founders of American Trotskyism. Shachtman by the 1950s had moved to a social democratic stance, and in the 1960s he and his followers, including Kahn, entered the Socialist party. From the Socialist party, Kahn entered the AFL-CIO and eventually succeeded to Lovestone's and Brown's position, pursuing their policies with enthusiasm and effectiveness.

In the 1970s and 1980s Brown and then Kahn continued to adhere to Lovestone's view that the key to stopping or reversing Communist influence abroad was the development of an independent non-Communist labor movement. In pursuit of this strategy the AFL-CIO subsidized the Solidarity labor movement in Poland that eventually brought down Poland's Communist regime. It also aided anti-Communist unions in Nicaragua that opposed the pro-Soviet Sandinista government.

Others of Lovestone's Communist party faction also made significant contributions to the anti-Communist cause. Bertram Wolfe, the CPUSA's representative to the Communist International in 1929, was expelled with Lovestone and became a leading figure in Lovestone's Communist Party (Opposition). When Lovestone turned to anti-Communist organizing in the labor movement, Wolfe turned to scholarship. He became a noted authority on Spanish-language literature and published several highly regarded studies of the radical Mexican muralist Diego Rivera. He also published many essays analyzing Soviet actions and warning of Stalin's ambitions. His 1948 book, *Three Who Made a Revolution*, on Lenin, Trotsky, and Stalin, was a scholarly triumph that dispersed much of the misinformation that had enveloped those three leaders. In the 1950s he headed the State Department's Ideological Advisory Unit that helped to plan U.S. cold war policies.

Benjamin Gitlow was one of the chief founders of the CPUSA and briefly its general secretary in 1929 before he was expelled for his support of Lovestone. He headed Lovestone's dissident Communist organization for several years but reached an anti-Communist position earlier than Lovestone and broke with him in 1933. Unlike Lovestone, who eventually moved to a democratic socialist position, Gitlow adopted a hard conservative stance that combined anticommunism with hostility to liberalism. His 1939 autobiography, *I Confess*, and his 1948 analysis of American communism, *The Whole of Their Lives*, revealed a great deal about the inner workings of the American Commu-

nist movement. Both books took the view that the CPUSA was essentially a Moscow-controlled fifth column. In making his case,
Gitlow's only evidence was his own memory of events or conver-
sations; in some instances this proved highly accurate, but in others it led him astray. A number of his controversial but
unverified charges, however, were later confirmed. For example,
in the late 1930s he charged that Margaret Browder, the sister of
the CPUSA's general secretary, worked for Soviet intelligence.
Journalists at the time and many historians dismissed Gitlow's
charge as an unsavory instance of character assassination. After
the collapse of Soviet communism, records found in Soviet
archives showed that Margaret Browder, with her brother's full
knowledge, had been employed by the Soviet Union's chief spy
agency.

The labor movement as a whole proved to be one of the strongest
institutional barriers to American communism. Even at the
height of communism's appeal, unions sympathetic to the Communist party or led by Communists represented only about one-
quarter of the CIO's members. Communists had at best only a
toehold in the larger AFL. Of the total labor movement, workers
in Communist-aligned unions represented less than a sixth of the
membership.

Of the five-sixths of organized labor that was non-Communist, a portion would best be described as indifferent to communism rather than hostile. The majority, however, was actively
hostile. Because the labor movement was a mass institution,
much of labor's anticommunism was simply a reflection of the
many anti-Communist currents in the broader society, such as
nationalistic or religious-based anticommunism. But the American labor movement also generated a unique anti-Communist
immunity of its own that derived from the basic ethos of American unionism. That ethos dated from the founding of the American Federation of Labor in 1886. Before that time American
workers in their labor organizations had tried a variety of ideologies: Jacksonian egalitarianism, producer cooperatives, fiat
money "greenbackism," violent anarchism and syndicalism, the

state socialism of Ferdinand Lassalle, and the revolutionary socialism of Karl Marx. In opposition to these approaches, the AFL's chief founder and long-time president Samuel Gompers espoused a philosophy of "wage consciousness" aimed at practical and immediate benefits for workers rather than the transformation of society. This "pure-and-simple" trade union philosophy rejected the Marxist concept of unions as chiefly weapons in a broader class war for control of the state and society. The AFL's wage consciousness fitted the situation of American workers much better than more ambitious and comprehensive philosophies such as Marxism. American workers were extraordinarily diverse, and Gompers's wage consciousness expressed one of the few common elements in the lives of otherwise very different workers. All of them wanted more and could understand the common need for higher wages and greater control over their jobs.

Gompers did not reject trade union participation in politics; rather he saw politics as an arena where trade unions would participate in order to defend themselves or advance their interests in a manner similar to that of other groups in American society. Gompers regarded the freewheeling pluralism of American democracy as made to order for independent unions that would reward their friends and punish their enemies in electoral competition. But he strenuously opposed the subordination of unions to political organizations and the politicizing of trade union goals. In Gompers's view, American society was so diverse and the American economy so complex that workers and particularly organized labor were not likely ever to constitute a controlling majority. In view of the unions' minority status, Gompers felt that the government would often be in the hands of those hostile or indifferent to labor. Consequently Gompers feared excessive government regulation of economic matters as a threat to the independent power of organized union workers. Socialism, with its program of nationalized property and government control of all aspects of the economy, was anathema to Gompers. Communism was thrice damned because it combined government control of the economy with the subordination of unions to a political party and a rejection of democracy. Gompers died in 1924, but the labor movement he founded largely embodied his philosophy.

In the mid-1930s the CIO not so much challenged as modified Gompers's legacy. Although the CIO rejected the AFL's preference for craft over industrial unionism, Gompers's basic philosophy regarding the relationship of the labor movement to society remained intact. CIO leaders took a broader view of the role of unions, welcomed the welfare state as an ally of workers, and were much more willing than the rival AFL to involve the CIO in partisan politics. But CIO leaders remained reluctant to subordinate the labor movement to a political party. Despite occasional rhetoric about sponsoring a labor party, CIO leaders saw the CIO's role as that of a powerful but autonomous member of the New Deal coalition.

The AFL, after its initial shock at the CIO insurgency, fought back in the late 1930s, often matching or exceeding the CIO in organizing new members and easily remaining larger than its younger rival. In the process the AFL moved toward the CIO's broader view of Gompers's legacy. Most AFL unions remained craft oriented, but many of the larger AFL unions began to interpret their craft lines so broadly that the structural distinction between an AFL union and a CIO union became a difference of degree rather than of kind. The largest AFL union, the Teamsters, paid almost no attention to craft lines in its organizational practices. AFL unions, while not as aggressive as the CIO's, also became more active in politics and, like the CIO, operated largely within the New Deal coalition and the Democratic party.

Most AFL and CIO leaders retained Gompers's basic attitude toward politics and politicians. They insisted on unions' autonomy—that the labor movement entered the political arena for its own reasons and to serve its own interests. The idea that unions should accept direction from a political body outside the union movement was anathema. It was this attitude that would bring about the destruction of the Communist position in the labor movement.

6

The Struggle for the Soul of American Liberalism

WHEN WORLD WAR II ENDED, American liberals and the Democratic party faced an uncertain future. Harry Truman had enjoyed only limited national standing before Roosevelt selected him for the vice-presidency in 1944, and most liberals and the CIO had resisted Roosevelt's decision to replace Henry Wallace on the ticket. After Roosevelt's death, Truman was initially unable to provide the Democratic party or liberalism with a renewed sense of direction and appeared to be a parochial politician out of his depth. Voters expressed their attitude in the midterm elections of 1946 by giving Republicans control of both houses of Congress.

With little leadership coming from the White House, other forces attempted to seize the initiative to renew the New Deal. Popular Front liberals appeared to be the strongest and most aggressive. They argued that conservative successes were the result of divisions among progressives rather than public dissatisfaction with the New Deal message, and that the correct course was one of organizational and political solidarity among liberals and with the labor movement. Popular Front liberals set about creating a nationwide political organization that, in alliance with the CIO's Political Action Committee, would have a decisive influence on the direction of the New Deal coalition. In late 1946 Popular Front liberals sponsored a General Conference of Progressives

that brought together hundreds of leading liberal political activists, prominent New Deal Democrats, and union leaders.
Among the sponsoring organizations were the National Citizens
Political Action Committee and the Independent Citizens Committee of the Arts, Sciences, and Professions.

The National Citizens Political Action Committee had been
created in 1944 as an auxiliary of the CIO's Political Action Committee; it was a vehicle to mobilize nonunion and professional
voters sympathetic to the New Deal. Popular Front supporters
did not control the CIO's Political Action Committee but they
were a major force in it, and when the National Citizens Political
Action Committee was spun off as an independent organization
it emerged as a thoroughly Popular Front body. Elmer Benson,
its chairman and a former U.S. senator and governor from Minnesota, was a firm ally of the Communist party. Concealed Communists made up a significant part of the National Citizens
Political Action Committee professional staff and regional leaders. The Independent Citizens Committee of the Arts, Sciences,
and Professions was a similar organization, originally formed as
a means for prominent Hollywood stars, artists, musicians, writers, and elite professionals to show their support for Roosevelt in
1944. After the General Conference of Progressives met, the National Citizens Political Action Committee and the Independent
Citizens Committee of the Arts, Sciences, and Professions
merged to form the Progressive Citizens of America with Elmer
Benson as its chairman.

Also sponsoring the 1946 General Conference was the CIO.
CIO head Philip Murray accepted the Popular Front argument
that liberal unity was the best strategy to protect the New Deal's
gains. It coincided with his internal CIO policy of unity that allied the CIO's Popular Front wing with his dominant centrist
bloc. When the Progressive Citizens of America formed, both
Murray and Jack Kroll, head of the CIO's Political Action Committee, accepted positions as vice-chairmen. As another sign of
the political appeal of the Popular Front agenda, A. F. Whitney
of the Brotherhood of Railway Trainmen also joined the Progressive Citizens' campaign. The rail brotherhoods, several of

which were independent of either the AFL or the CIO, were in that era politically formidable; they were also engaged in an angry quarrel with the Truman administration over its efforts to block a postwar rail strike that threatened to disrupt the economy. Another sponsor of the General Conference of Progressives was the National Farmers Union and its leader, James Patton. Although not the largest farm organization, the National Farmers Union was strong in the Midwest and could count enclaves of support in a few Eastern states. It had been an enthusiastic backer of the New Deal, and its economically powerful network of farm cooperatives was closely tied to the federal government's agricultural programs.

The Progressive Citizens of America presented a formidable coalition: fifty thousand politically active members, a network of state and local affiliates, and an alliance with the CIO, the rail brotherhoods, and the National Farmers Union. Given President Truman's political weakness, the coalition appeared to have the potential to dominate liberal politics in the postwar era.

Popular Front leadership of the Progressive Citizens of America came with a price. Popular Front liberals emphasized that in achieving liberal unity two items could not be compromised. First, liberals must support a foreign policy that accommodated Stalin's postwar goals. Neither the Soviet Union's internal policies nor Soviet domination of the peoples of Eastern and Central Europe could be criticized. Nor should the United States support China's Nationalist government that was losing ground to the forces of the Chinese Communist party under Mao Tse-tung. Second, the concealed role of American Communists within the liberal and labor movements was not to be publicly discussed or criticized. To do so was considered "red-baiting," a term of ultimate political opprobrium in Popular Front eyes.

The only liberal organization to contest the direction chosen by the General Conference of Progressives was the tiny Union for Democratic Action. Formed in 1940, the Union brought elements of the left-wing anti-Communist tradition into the mainstream of American liberalism. Most of the Union for Democratic Action's founders were Socialists who had come to regard the Socialist party as ineffective and who saw in the New Deal an American social democratic movement. Among the Union's founders were Andrew Biemiller, a Socialist party activist, AFL organizer, and state legislator in Wisconsin; Murray Gross and Gus Tyler of the International Ladies Garment Workers Union; James Carey, president of the CIO's United Electrical Workers, who had severed relations with his union's dominant Communist faction after the Nazi-Soviet pact; Alfred Bingham, editor of the left-liberal journal *Common Sense* and a critic of Popular Front liberalism; and James Loeb, a Socialist who had been in Spain during its civil war, an experience that had made him a lifelong enemy of communism. Loeb became the Union for Democratic Action's full-time director and organizer. The Union's first chairman was Freda Kirchwey, owner and editor of *The Nation* and a former Popular Front enthusiast then alienated from the Communists by the Nazi-Soviet pact.

The founders of the Union for Democratic Action had in common a package of political convictions. While most were Socialist in principle, all by 1940 had become supporters of Roosevelt's New Deal and saw its reformist, interest-group liberalism as the only practical path for left-of-center politics. All were also internationalists who felt that the United States had a responsibility to promote democracy abroad and, in particular, to resist the spread of Nazism and fascism. All of them had also concluded that supporters of democracy could not work with Communists. Some had always held this as a matter of principle, others had reached the judgment only after experience in Popular Front politics and the reality of the Nazi-Soviet pact left them no other choice. The disarray that the Nazi-Soviet pact caused to Popular Front liberalism allowed the Union for Democratic Action quickly to carve out a niche for itself as the only liberal-left group that was simultaneously anti-Nazi, anti-Communist, and in firm support of Roosevelt's foreign and domestic policies.

Once Nazi Germany attacked the Soviet Union and the United States joined the war, however, anticommunism became a liability on the liberal left. The Roosevelt administration, which had welcomed the organization of the Union for Democratic Action in 1940, in 1942 wanted the broadest possible coalition behind its war policies and regarded Popular Front liberalism as its ally. Although the anti-Communist wing of the CIO gave the Union for Democratic Action some support, the CIO's centrist leaders such as Philip Murray kept it at arm's length, not wishing to offend the CIO's powerful Communist-led left wing. Most major liberal journals, such as *The Nation* and the *New Republic*, which had cheered the Union for Democratic Action in 1940 and 1941, drifted back to a Popular Front stance.

The Union for Democratic Action survived to the end of World War II, but only barely. Its finances were precarious and its membership small, a claimed ten thousand but probably many fewer. It was dwarfed by liberal organizations that adhered to a Popular Front line. Yet the Union for Democratic Action, despite its size and lack of funding, was organizational home for a political stance that came to dominate the Democratic party after World War II.

Part of this success can be credited to a very unlikely source, a Lutheran theologian named Reinhold Niebuhr. Niebuhr had attended Yale University's Divinity School where he ingested the modernist and Social Gospel theology that was standard among mainstream American Protestants. Niebuhr's experience as pastor of a working-class Detroit church and his reaction to World War I provoked him to a radical change of stance. Deciding that liberal Christianity's optimism about human nature was unsound, he shifted toward an older orthodox biblical theology that put man's imperfectibility at the center of the Christian worldview. With this he fused the Social Gospel movement's view that the Christian mission was not only with individual salvation but with social redemption. Niebuhr called his stance "Christian realism." His growing reputation as an analyst of social problems from a Christian perspective brought him in 1928 to a lecturer's position in Christian social ethics at New York's Union Theological Seminary. His books, *Moral Man and Immoral Society* (1932), *The Nature and Destiny of Man* (1941), and *Children of Light, Children of Darkness* (1944) established his reputation as a Christian thinker on political and social ethics.

In the 1920s and early 1930s, the political views Niebuhr derived from his theology were characterized by pacifism and radical socialism. The rise of Nazism and the coming of World War II caused him to rethink his political program, and in 1940 he left the Socialist party because of its pacifist opposition to American participation in the war against Nazi Germany, and joined the Union for Democratic Action.

Niebuhr's views and ideas resonated with many in the Union for Democratic Action because he offered liberals an attractive insight into human nature. Niebuhr's views appealed to those who had given up on the complacent optimism of traditional American reformism and who yet sought a third way between the black evil of Nazism and the demonic idealism of Stalin's communism. In Niebuhr's view, modern liberalism lacked an understanding of mankind's flawed nature; in Christian terms, liberal civilization did not recognize the corruption that humanity's original sin had inflicted on human nature. Niebuhr declared that liberalism's blindness to the role of the will-to-power in human life dangerously weakened it against an external foe such as Nazism and facilitated liberalism's internal corruption, for human self-interest inevitably manipulated idealism. Niebuhr viewed communism as the ultimate corruption of idealism; because communism lacked any sense of humanity's limitations, Niebuhr saw its dreams of socialist harmony becoming an instrument of a new Stalinist ruling class in the Soviet Union, one that used idealistic goals to give moral sanction to an unlimited and corrupted will-to-power.

Niebuhr called for an injection of Christian realism into liberal theory. Any reform enterprise that did not take into account mankind's crippled capacity for good, he believed, would inevitably fall to internal corruption. Niebuhr argued that democracy's limitations on state power and its legitimation of dissent and political opposition offered the only effective check on the tendency of rulers, no matter how well motivated, toward greed, selfishness, and abuse of power.

As World War II ended and the cold war began, Niebuhr's views appealed to a rising generation of liberal activists. The

Popular Front's simple division of the world between evil fascists and good progressives was inadequate to deal with Stalin's purges, the Nazi-Soviet pact, and after 1945 the Soviet suppression of democratic forces in Eastern Europe.

Arthur M. Schlesinger, Jr., the Harvard historian who had served in the Office of Strategic Services during World War II, offered a secularized version of Niebuhr's views in what he called "vital center" liberalism. First in an influential article in the mass-circulation *Life* magazine, and in 1949 in a book entitled *The Vital Center*, Schlesinger called on liberals to see the world as complex, with deadly threats to democracy coming from the left as well as the right, and requiring difficult moral decisions between greater and lesser evils. Schlesinger's "vital center" liberalism used a virile, pugnacious rhetoric that appealed to liberal war veterans shaped by the masculine ethos of war. There was throughout Schlesinger's rhetoric a strong note of contempt for the claims of moral purity and utopian idealism that were hallmarks of Popular Front rhetoric.

When the Union for Democratic Action challenged the General Conference of Progressives, it was a David-versus-Goliath contest. The Union had less than a fifth as many members as the Progressive Citizens, had nothing resembling its CIO backing, and was in chronic financial difficulty. Despite this, Union leaders refused to endorse the 1946 General Conference of Progressives and in early 1947 held their own meeting in Washington. The Union renamed itself Americans for Democratic Action (ADA) and launched a drive to establish itself as the nation's leading liberal body.

The new Americans for Democratic Action, though small, included a formidable array of talent. The leading figures at its founding conference were Reinhold Niebuhr, Arthur Schlesinger, Jr., Joseph Rauh (a former New Deal attorney just beginning a career as a leading civil rights lawyer), and prominent New Deal figures such as Elmer Davis, an influential radio commentator and former head of the Office of War Information; Leon Henderson, former chief of the wartime Office of Price Administration; the economist John Kenneth Galbraith; and,

most notably, Eleanor Roosevelt and Franklin D. Roosevelt, Jr.,
President Roosevelt's widow and son. Mrs. Roosevelt had been a
Popular Front favorite in the late 1930s, but she had come to mistrust Communists after the Nazi-Soviet pact, and as a U.S. delegate to the United Nations in 1946 had developed a profound
antipathy for the aggressive bullying tactics of Soviet diplomacy.
Representing the anti-Communist wing of the labor movement
were Walter Reuther of the United Auto Workers, James Carey
of the United Electrical Workers, and Emil Reeve of the Textile
Workers Union of America (three leading CIO anti-Communists), as well as David Dubinsky of the International Ladies
Garment Workers Union and Hugo Ernst of the Hotel and
Restaurant Employees union (two prominent AFL anti-Communists). Also at the founding ADA conference were young liberal politicians with ambitions for public office, including
Hubert Humphrey, mayor of Minneapolis, and Chester Bowles,
an aspiring political figure in Connecticut.

Both the Americans for Democratic Action and the Progressive Citizens of America claimed to embody the authentic spirit
of the New Deal. Both advocated similar programs of domestic
reform based on New Deal precedents: an expanding regulatory
state, increased government planning, centralization of government power at the federal level, and expanded social welfare
benefits. Neither organization openly advocated economic col-
lectivism or socialism, though both included people who hoped
that the New Deal's welfare state would open the way to full-
fledged socialism. Both also brought to the fore an item that
the New Deal had muted: equal rights for black Americans.
Both organizations made opposition to racial segregation a leading demand. Of the two, the ADA had the strongest tie to black
Americans through its close links to the National Association for
the Advancement of Colored Peoples (NAACP), the nation's
largest black-oriented advocacy group. Walter White, national
director of the NAACP, served on the organizing committee of the
ADA's founding convention. The Progressive Citizens, however,
through their Communist ties, also rightly claimed a role as civil
rights pioneers. Communist-led CIO unions were noticeably

more aggressive than others in championing equal treatment for black workers, and the CPUSA itself had long made black rights a priority.

Where Americans for Democratic Action and the Progressive Citizens of America differed most was on foreign policy. Each claimed to be continuing in the postwar period the policies that Roosevelt had pursued during the war. The Progressive Citizens of America asserted that the bedrock of American foreign policy must be the continuation of the wartime alliance with the Soviet Union. This required recognizing the justice of Soviet predominance in Eastern and Central Europe, Soviet claims on northern Iran, and refraining from aligning the nations of Western Europe in an anti-Soviet bloc. Only such a policy of friendship and accommodation toward the Soviet Union would assure peace.

ADA leaders saw Roosevelt's wartime policy in a different light; they regarded the wartime alliance with the Soviet Union as having been a means to an end, not an end in itself. The end was the immediate goal of defeating Nazi Germany and a more general one of promoting democracy world-wide. This latter goal had been an explicit American and liberal war aim, enunciated in the Atlantic Charter, Roosevelt's Four Freedoms speeches, and the Yalta Conference Declaration for the Liberation of Europe. These proclamations stated that the war was being fought in order to free the oppressed peoples of Europe from tyranny and assure them of national independence and democratic self-rule. In the eyes of ADA liberals, replacing Nazi tyranny in Eastern Europe with Communist tyranny was not what the war had been about.

While both the Progressive Citizens of America and the Americans for Democratic Action attracted New Deal veterans, the ADA also attracted a number of new faces, young politicians who had been shaped and inspired by the New Deal but who had been too young to play a major role. One such was Hubert Humphrey. In 1944 he helped bring about the merger of Minnesota's two liberal parties, the Farmer-Labor party and the Democratic party, to form the Democratic-Farmer-Labor party (DFL), which remains the name of Minnesota's Democratic party to this day. With unified liberal support, he ran and won the Minneapolis mayoralty in 1945. Although Minneapolis had a "weak mayor" system of government, Humphrey's barnstorming style of leadership allowed him to fashion a workable majority on the city council and to reform city services. In particular, Humphrey attracted national attention with his pioneering efforts in civil rights.

Humphrey was the first attractive campaigner to appear on the liberal horizon in Minnesota since Floyd B. Olson had established the Farmer-Labor party's dominance of the state in the early 1930s. With his reputation established and a solid political base in Minneapolis, Humphrey was ready to move up to statewide office in 1946. He had also gathered around him a core of talented young liberals, mostly veterans of World War II, who shared his ambition and vision of a revived New Deal liberalism reshaped to deal with postwar problems. Humphrey's rise, however, received an unexpected check.

The Democratic-Farmer-Labor party had within it a strong Popular Front faction that had come into the merged party with its Farmer-Labor element. Humphrey had not opposed this group; his attitude had been one of indifference. Oriented toward a pragmatic liberalism, Humphrey habitually avoided ideological confrontation and sought to make the Democratic party an inclusive coalition that stretched from the broad center to the left of American politics. With his Democratic party background, he knew little of the vicious fights between anti-Communist and Popular Front supporters that had rent the Farmer-Labor party in the late 1930s and early 1940s. When the two parties merged in 1944, Popular Front liberals were supporting Roosevelt, and there was no occasion for direct conflict.

Humphrey and his allies fully expected to control the 1946 DFL state convention and believed that DFL backing for either the governorship or a U.S. Senate seat was Humphrey's for the asking. The DFL's Popular Front faction was of a different mind. Its chief was Elmer Benson, former U.S. senator and Minnesota governor who was national chairman of the National Citizens Political Action Committee, shortly to become the Progressive Citizens of America. It included veteran Farmer-Labor Popular Front tacticians Orville Olson, state chairman of the Minnesota affiliate of the National Citizens Political Action Committee, and John Jacobson, director of the Minnesota CIO's Political Action Committee. Both were secret members of the Communist party.

When the 1946 Minnesota DFL convention met, the Popular Front faction held only a minority of the delegates, but it was united and aggressive. Humphrey, presenting himself as a non-factional leader, refused to respond to the Popular Front argument that it represented a pure, uncompromised New Deal stance and that President Truman was betraying Roosevelt's policies by failing to find common ground with Stalin. Humphrey ignored the warnings from former Farmer-Labor anti-Communists, veterans of a long and ultimately losing factional fight, that failing to confront the Popular Front faction on an ideological basis was a mistake.

Given Humphrey's stance, most of the convention was without ideological coherence and vulnerable to the aggressive tactics of the Popular Front minority. The latter outmaneuvered Humphrey, split the majority, and elected a DFL party chairman beholden to them and a party executive committee controlled by Elmer Benson. Triumphant Popular Front leaders told Humphrey he could have the nomination for senator or governor, but only if he accepted Popular Front control of his campaign. Humphrey refused and left the convention with his hopes of a quick rise to high office shattered.

Shortly after this James Loeb, director of the Union for Democratic Action, published a long letter in the *New Republic*. In it he argued that a revival of liberalism depended on severing the link in the public mind between liberals and Soviet tyranny that had been established by the Popular Front's calls for accommodating Stalin's ambitions in Europe. Liberal cooperation with American Communists was, Loeb charged, a moral betrayal of democratic values. One of Humphrey's advisers saw the letter's relevance to Humphrey's predicament and convinced Loeb to meet with Humphrey. The meeting clarified Humphrey's thinking. Humphrey adopted a forthright anti-Communist liberal stance, and he and the young liberals who surrounded him participated in the founding convention of the Americans for Democratic Action.

The next two years were among the most contested in the history of Minnesota liberalism and mirrored the national battle between Popular Front and anti-Communist liberals. As was true nationally, in its early stages Popular Front liberals were institutionally stronger, controlling the state leadership of the Democratic-Farmer-Labor party, the Minnesota affiliate of the Progressive Citizens of America, and the Minnesota CIO's Political Action Committee.

In late 1947 Henry Wallace announced that he would run for president on a platform that combined a domestic program for a revived New Deal with a foreign policy that replaced Truman's resistance to Soviet expansion with one seeking cooperation with Stalin. Rather than challenge Truman for the Democratic nomination, Wallace announced he would transform the Progressive Citizens of America into a new "Progressive party" and seek to replace the Democrats as the main rival to the Republicans. Elmer Benson, who became the first national chairman of the Progressive party, immediately announced that when the DFL state convention met in 1948 it would vote to disaffiliate from the Democratic party and become the state affiliate of the Progressive party.

Having easily defeated Humphrey in 1946, Benson and his "progressives," as Popular Front liberals increasingly called themselves, badly underestimated him. Defining Communists and their allies as illegitimate participants in the liberal coalition, Humphrey forged a coherent anti-Communist faction whose discipline and tactical skill—thanks to his close friend Orville Freeman—was a match for the veterans of the Popular Front. Freeman, a Marine combat officer, had taken a position handling veterans affairs for Mayor Humphrey when he returned from the war. He also organized the Minnesota chapter of the American Veterans Committee and led the faction that resisted demands that the American Veterans Committee oppose Truman's foreign policy. Freeman's fight was successful, and he brought the network of veterans that had gathered around him into the fight for control of the DFL party.

Several other factors aided the anti-Communist campaign of Humphrey and Freeman. Minnesota's AFL unions were overwhelmingly anti-Communist but as a result of sour experiences with the Farmer-Labor party in the 1930s had largely withdrawn from partisan politics. Congressional passage of the Taft-Hartley Act in 1947, however, with its perceived antilabor provisions, sparked a political revival in the AFL, and its leaders mobilized their members to punish the Republicans in 1948. In Minnesota, AFL leaders threw their considerable support in personnel and money behind Humphrey and his faction. The passage of Taft-Hartley also encouraged national CIO leaders to decide that the power of the CIO's Popular Front wing was a threat to the CIO's long-run institutional interests. Once the national leadership of the CIO shifted to an aggressive anti-Communist stance, several major Minnesota CIO leaders who had supported Communist control of the Minnesota CIO shifted to the anti-Communist camp. By mid-1948 John Jacobson, the secret Communist who headed the Minnesota CIO's Political Action Committee, was forced out. The Minnesota CIO was transformed from the principal financier and supporter of Popular Front control of the DFL into an enthusiastic supporter of Humphrey and his anti-Communist faction.

In similar fashion, Minnesota's numerous farm cooperatives also enlisted in Humphrey's campaign. They had once been a pillar of the Farmer-Labor party but, like the AFL, had largely withdrawn from partisan politics by the end of the 1930s because of the disruption that Farmer-Labor factionalism was causing within the farm coop movement. The coops' political passivity, however, was also shaken by Republicans in 1947, in this case by prospects that a Republican president and a Republican-controlled Congress would abolish the favorable tax treatment that farm cooperatives received. Minnesota farm cooperatives decided that their institutional interests required a Democratic victory in 1948, and that Humphrey was the best prospect for bringing Minnesota into the Democratic column. They too threw in their lot with Humphrey and his anti-Communist campaign.

The contest for the allegiance of Minnesota liberals was hard fought and vituperative. Humphrey hammered away at the impropriety of liberals maintaining a political relationship with a group as profoundly anti-democratic as the Communists. Progressives found it difficult to respond directly to these attacks because the Minnesota campaign leaders for Wallace whom Humphrey and Freeman named as concealed Communists actually *were* Communists and were known as such by too many DFL activists for indignant denials to have any punch. With the press filled with news of the Communist coup in Czechoslovakia and Stalin's attempt to starve West Berlin into submission, the Progressives' unwavering defense of Soviet foreign policy rang increasingly hollow.

In the DFL caucuses in the spring of 1948, Humphrey's forces won decisive majorities in most counties. Wallace supporters who had been elected as state DFL delegates now withdrew and held a rival state convention proclaiming that the Humphrey forces had stolen the caucuses. But in the DFL primary, candidates endorsed by the pro-Humphrey DFL convention overwhelmed those of the pro-Wallace DFL convention; in the primary for the DFL nomination for the U.S. Senate, Humphrey defeated his Progressive rival by a margin of eight to one. After their primary defeat, the pro-Wallace DFL faction reorganized themselves as the Minnesota Progressive party and placed a slate of candidates on the ballot. The general election completed the destruction of the once-strong Popular Front faction in Minnesota politics. Wallace received only 2.3 percent of Minnesota's vote, while the Progressive candidate for governor (a secret member of the Communist party) fared little better, just under 3 percent. Meanwhile, the DFL under the leadership of Humphrey and Freeman (the new DFL state chairman) scored its largest-ever electoral victory. Truman won Minnesota's presidential vote, Humphrey defeated the incumbent Republican U.S. senator by a landslide, and the DFL won four U.S. House seats (having won only one in 1946).

This 1947–1948 struggle was the shaping event for a generation of Minnesota liberals who took the lessons into national politics. In addition to his long service as a U.S. senator, Humphrey
was vice-president and the Democratic presidential candidate in
1968. Freeman became governor and served in the cabinets of
presidents Kennedy and Johnson. Eugene McCarthy vaulted
into the U.S. House in 1948 through his leadership of the anti-
Communist bloc of the Ramsey County (St. Paul) DFL party.
McCarthy later won election to the U.S. Senate and contended
for the Democratic presidential nomination in 1968. Walter
Mondale helped the Humphrey faction take over the DFL youth
affiliate and in 1948 served as one of Freeman's aides. He later
became a U.S. senator, vice-president, and Democratic presidential candidate in 1976.

Patterns of politics similar to those in Minnesota occurred in
other states as well. The American Labor party, the New York
affiliate of the Progressive party, went into the 1948 election with
two incumbent congressmen and high hopes for a strong showing, but this contest began the party's slide into ruin. Representative Leo Isacson, one of the ALP incumbents, lost to a Democrat;
the other incumbent, Representative Vito Marcantonio, won reelection by only a narrow plurality of 37 percent in a three-way
race. In 1950 the Democratic, Republican, and Liberal parties in
New York united behind a single candidate and defeated Marcantonio. Also in 1950 the Liberal party, founded by anti-Communists who had left the ALP, surpassed the ALP in every
contest and became the leading third party in New York. By
1952 the once powerful ALP had ceased to be a significant force.

In Washington state the Popular Front–aligned Washington
Commonwealth Federation had become a major factor in the
state Democratic party in the late 1930s and early 1940s; in 1944
its head, Hugh DeLacy won election to Congress as a Democrat.
In 1945 the Commonwealth Federation dissolved, announcing
that its style of politics was now well integrated into the Democratic party. Once the cold war began, however, an acrimonious
fight erupted between Popular Front liberals and anti-Communist liberals, the latter led by Democratic congressman Henry

Jackson. In 1948 DeLacy resurrected the Commonwealth Federation constituency as the basis for the Washington state Progressive party. After the Progressives did poorly in the 1948 election,
the organization drifted into insignificance.

In Wisconsin Frank Hoan, the long-time Socialist mayor of
Milwaukee, became a Democrat during World War II and
brought many of the Wisconsin Socialist party's anti-Communist
activists into the Democratic party with him. In 1946 Hoan engi-
neered the repudiation by major Democrats of the congressional
candidacy of Edmund Bobrowicz, a Popular Front–aligned Fur
and Leather Workers official who had won the Democratic
nomination in a Milwaukee district. In addition to this infusion
of older anti-Communist Socialists, a group of young liberals in
the anti-Communist faction of the American Veterans Committee, led by Gaylord Nelson and Henry Reuss, entered the party.
In 1948 Nelson and Reuss formed the Democratic Organizing
Committee which became the most powerful organization
within the Wisconsin Democratic party. Nelson later won election as governor and U.S. senator while Reuss became a longtime
congressman.

The fight between Popular Front Progressives and anti-Communist liberals at the state level was duplicated nationally in the
struggle between the Americans for Democratic Action and the
Progressive Citizens of America. The latter started with many
times more members, the endorsement of major liberal spokesmen and Hollywood celebrities, financial and manpower support from the Popular Front wing of the CIO, and the covert
backing of the CPUSA. In 1948 the ADA hired Andrew Biemiller
as its political director. Biemiller was a superb choice. A former
member of Congress, he had served for years as an AFL organizer and political operative in Wisconsin and was a veteran of
the long fight waged by the AFL in alliance with anti-Communist Socialists to prevent Communist control of Wisconsin's Progressive party in the 1930s. In that role Biemiller had gone up
directly against Eugene Dennis, then head of the Wisconsin
Communist party, who had forged a powerful Popular Front

faction in Wisconsin. In 1948 Dennis was general secretary of the CPUSA and directly supervised its covert role in Wallace's Progressive party. Biemiller, who was known and trusted by anti-Communist CIO officials as well as by AFL leaders, was able to coordinate the ADA's activities with the massive political mobilization undertaken by the AFL and the CIO in 1948. The resulting coherence vastly enhanced the power of the anti-Communist message in liberal circles.

Biemiller teamed up with Hubert Humphrey at the 1948 Democratic National Convention to pull off one of that year's political triumphs. The Democratic convention had begun as a lackluster affair because President Truman's public support was extremely low. The general view was that he was a sure loser in the fall election. Under Humphrey's leadership, liberal delegates made a floor fight for a strong civil rights plank. The fight electrified a listless convention, and Humphrey's passionate speech for equal rights for black Americans, carried nationwide on radio, was one of the convention's emotional highlights. It also sparked Southern delegates to walk out of the convention and form the segregationist States Rights party behind the presidential candidacy of Governor J. Strom Thurmond of South Carolina. The passage of the plank itself was a milestone marking the emergence of civil rights as a major political issue. Humphrey, the Americans for Democratic Action, and the anti-Communist liberalism they espoused drew high praise in liberal circles for the passage of the civil rights plank.

The Democratic convention also saw the reversal of Truman's fortunes. To the surprise of the convention delegates and the national radio audience that heard him, the president delivered an aggressive, fighting acceptance speech that brought the dispirited Democrats to their feet cheering. Truman followed up the convention with a series of hard-hitting speeches successfully painting the Republican-controlled congress as a "do-nothing" body and presenting himself as the protector of the welfare gains brought about by the New Deal.

Although most ADA leaders and members were unhappy with Truman, the president's campaign needs and ADA goals coincided: both wanted the Wallace campaign and his Progressive party to fail, and fail badly. The result was a de facto alliance between the White House and the Americans for Democratic Action that started out chilly but grew warmer by the fall of 1948. Truman did not wish to take on Wallace directly, because to do so would raise Wallace's credibility and accept his premise that the two were competing for the leadership of American liberalism. Instead Truman concentrated his attacks on the Republicans while leaving the ADA to discredit Wallace among liberals and counting on the labor movement to deny the Progressive party the funds and manpower it needed for a viable campaign.

The ADA succeeded in destroying Wallace's position among liberal voters, but they were helped by international events and missteps by the candidate and his party. The Progressives' national convention reinforced Wallace's image as a Soviet apologist by approving a platform that placed all the blame for Soviet-American tensions on the United States. The ADA exploited this mistake by ensuring that liberals learned of the fate of an amendment to the Progressive platform. The Vermont delegation had sought to dilute the lopsided pro-Soviet stance by suggesting a sentence stating: "Although we are critical of the present foreign policy of the United States, it is not our intention to give blanket endorsement to the foreign policy of any other nation." On its face this was innocuous, but to the reflexively pro-Soviet convention it hinted that Stalin's policies might be open to criticism. Progressive party leaders denounced the amendment and it went down to overwhelming defeat.

The Americans for Democratic Action circulated among liberals lengthy position papers, complete with quotes from speeches by Wallace or other high Progressive officials, examining Wallace's support for Soviet foreign policy positions and the role of concealed Communists in the Progressive party. These attacks forced non-Communists in the party to confront an issue that many had preferred to ignore, and resulted in a steady dropout of non-Communists who had initially joined the Wallace campaign. By the time of the general election, the Progressive party had been reduced to the Communists and their closest allies, a few Communist-aligned unions, a collection of political mavericks and chronic malcontents, and a scattering of Hollywood celebrities.

One of the decisive events in the victory of anti-Communist liberalism was the shift of the CIO to an aggressively anti-Communist stance. In 1946 Philip Murray, though hostile to communism, nonetheless tolerated the Communist wing of the CIO and accepted the postwar political strategy of Popular Front liberals. But starting in 1947 events inside and outside the CIO put enormous pressure on Murray's policy and eventually persuaded him to make certain basic choices.

One factor was the increasing strength of CIO anti-Communists. Since the 1930s Communists had been partners (though not controlling ones) in the ruling coalition in the United Auto Workers, the CIO's largest and most dynamic union. The chief opponent of the ruling group was Walter Reuther. Reuther came from a Socialist party background but in the early days of the CIO had been willing to work with Communists. As the CIO evolved, however, Reuther soured on the Communists; by the end of World War II he was their chief opponent. Behind Reuther was a diverse coalition of his personal followers along with Socialists, ACTU militants, followers of Max Shachtman, Trotskyists, and others who mistrusted the Communists. Reuther won the union presidency in 1946, but the coalition of which the Communists were a part retained control of the United Auto Workers' executive board and limited the impact of Reuther's victory. At the November 1947 auto workers' convention, however, Reuther's caucus routed its opponents. Reuther thereupon fired dozens of Communists from the union's staff and set about eliminating Communists from offices in UAW locals. Another major ally of the Communist party, Joseph Curran, president of the CIO's National Maritime Union (East and Gulf Coast sailors), also broke with the Communists at this time. In 1947 Curran and his supporters won control of the union and drove out the once-dominant Communist faction.

Passage of the Taft-Hartley Act by the Republican Congress in 1947 created the decisive conditions for Murray's abandonment of his unity policies. Taft-Hartley significantly reduced protections accorded unions under the National Labor Relations Act. AFL and CIO leaders were panicked and enraged by the law's restrictions on union power, and recognized the importance of the 1948 election. Truman's veto, though overridden, was a major step in his rebuilding of labor enthusiasm for his candidacy. If a Republican won the presidency and Congress stayed Republican, the union movement faced the passage of even harsher legislation. The modern labor movement, created in the 1930s under the legal protection of the National Labor Relations Act, was now at risk. To Philip Murray and to most labor leaders, defeating the Republican presidential candidate and unseating the Republican majorities in Congress was not simply desirable, it was fundamental in heading off a crippling attack on the labor movement.

Henry Wallace's presidential candidacy and the creation of the Progressive party was a potential disaster for labor. If the New Deal coalition split between Wallace and Truman, a Republican victory was assured. Murray was well aware that Communists were the driving force behind Wallace's decision to form the Progressive party. Shortly after this decision, Murray set about ejecting Communists from the labor movement. In January 1948 the CIO executive board voted by more than two to one to oppose the Progressive party movement. Although the resolution did not bind individual CIO unions, it bound the CIO's national staff as well as state and local CIO central bodies, and Murray eliminated Progressive party supporters (mostly Communists) from these offices. For example, Murray told Lee Pressman, the CIO's longtime general counsel and a concealed Communist, to make a choice: the CIO or the CPUSA. Pressman chose the CPUSA, resigned his post, and went to work for the Progressive party.

CIO anti-Communists had often told CIO centrists that Communists could not be trusted, that if Communist politics and union needs clashed, CIO Communists would put communism before the CIO. Until the late 1940s Communist politics and

CIO needs had generally coincided. But the Wallace campaign threatened the CIO's drive to defeat the Republicans in 1948. The CIO's anti-Communist faction and Murray's centrist bloc now became one, and the CIO split between an anti-Communist majority that encompassed unions with more than three-quarters of its membership, and a shrinking Communist-aligned minority.

The Communists and their allies in the CIO fought every step of the way. In every state and city CIO central body, Popular Front forces resisted the anti-Wallace order, refused to implement it, or ignored it. This only further angered Murray and reinforced his determination that the Communist role in the CIO must end. CIO officials quickly ousted Communists from their once powerful role in the CIO's Political Action Committee. In some cases the national CIO withdrew financial support from a defiant central body and directed CIO unions to treat a compliant local CIO Political Action Committee office as the de facto CIO central body. In other cases Murray pulled the central body's charter and formed an entirely new CIO organization. In New York City, for example, the CIO formed a new CIO regional body rather than attempt to reform the one that was Communist dominated. The CIO and the Amalgamated Clothing Workers also withdrew their support for the American Labor party, which had become the New York affiliate of Wallace's Progressive party. Deprived of union support, the American Labor party was soon overtaken by its rival, the anti-Communist Liberal party, as the political instrument of New York liberal-left voters.

Murray's decision to break the Communist position in the labor movement was a body blow to Popular Front liberalism and to the Communist party itself. Many events and personalities combined to destroy the effectiveness of American communism, but this was the single most damaging act. The Communist role in the CIO, in its central bodies, and in the CIO's Political Action Committee provided the backbone for the entire Popular Front wing of liberalism. CIO money, manpower, and endorsement meant political clout. Liberal officeholders wanted it and liberal candidates sought it. Conservative politicians feared it, and in

many closely contested elections even Republicans sought to pro-
pitiate the CIO. For many years this CIO support had given Popular Front liberals standing and influence. In 1948 Murray not
only removed CIO support from the Popular Front, he shifted
CIO resources to anti-Communist liberals. Before Murray acted,
Wallace and the Progressive party looked as if they might be a
decisive influence in American politics. Afterward, the Progressive campaign began to shrink.

   Murray's assaults on Communist enclaves in the CIO continued after the 1948 election. The 1949 national CIO convention
denounced the United Electrical Workers, largest of the Communist-led unions, as "the Communist Party masquerading as a
labor union" and charged that it had "assumed its true role as a
fifth column." The CIO ordered its Communist-aligned unions
to reform or face expulsion. Several did throw off Communist
leadership. When the clash came between Philip Murray and the
Communists, initially Mike Quill, president of the Transport
Workers Union and a concealed Communist, carried out the
CPUSA's orders. He supported Wallace and as a member of the
CIO's executive board voted against the anti–Progressive party
resolution. After the New York Communist party opposed a
subway fare increase that would finance a wage increase for his
union's members, however, Quill had enough. Announcing that
he put "wages before Wallace," he publicly resigned from the
American Labor party, privately quit the CPUSA, and forced
Communists out of their dominant role in his union.

   In eleven unions, however, Communist-aligned leaders held
firm and were either expelled or walked out of the CIO. The
eleven were the United Electrical Workers; Farm Equipment
Workers; International Union of Mine, Mill and Smelter Workers; International Longshoremen's and Warehousemen's Union;
National Union of Marine Cooks and Stewards; International
Fishermen and Allied Workers; Food, Tobacco, Agricultural
and Allied Workers; United Office and Professional Workers;
International Fur and Leather Workers Union; American Com-
munications Association; and the United Public Workers.

   The CIO authorized its affiliates to raid the expelled unions or

chartered new anti-Communist affiliates to take over their juris-
dictions. AFL unions also raided the weakened Communist-
aligned unions. Harry Bridges's International Longshoremen's
and Warehousemen's Union withstood anti-Communist assaults
almost without loss, and the Furriers did almost as well. But they
were exceptions. The United Electrical Workers, largest of the
Communist unions, survived but lost more than half its members to the newly chartered CIO International Union of Electrical Workers and to other AFL and CIO unions. The smaller
Communist-aligned unions were picked apart by AFL and CIO
raids and reduced to remnants.

The Taft-Hartley Act also struck at the power of concealed
Communists by requiring leaders of unions desiring the protection of federal law to sign non-Communist oaths. If Communist
union officials did not sign, their unions would lose National
Labor Relations Board protection, and most unions did not wish
to face employers without it. Communists could resign from the
Communist party, sign the oath, and keep their offices. But their
resignation needed to be total or they would face prosecution for
falsely signing the oath. The head of the Marine Cooks and
Stewards Union, for example, signed the oath but was convicted
of perjury when he failed to convince a court that he had in fact
left the Communist movement.

By the mid-1950s membership in the surviving Communist-
aligned unions numbered about 200,000, a fraction of the
1,370,000 members of the CIO's Communist-led faction at the
end of World War II.

The ejection of Communists from the CIO and the victory of
anti-Communist liberalism over Popular Front liberalism were
important, even decisive, events of the anti-Communist era.
They destroyed the Communist position in the CIO and thereby
removed American communism's chief domestic source of institutional support and legitimacy. Communist-aligned unions had
provided the CPUSA with hundreds of union staff jobs for Communist activists as well as union subsidies and endorsement for
Communist-backed causes. The victory of anti-Communist liberalism within the Democratic party and the liberal community

drastically narrowed the ability of Communists to operate within American society. Communists had not become a political factor by operating under their own banner; much of their influence came from their ability to influence established institutions of political liberalism. Once outside the protection provided by mainstream labor and liberal institutions, American communism faced isolation and near annihilation.

Had Communists not been ejected from the labor movement and the Democratic party, those institutions would likely have suffered deep wounds. By the late 1940s popular anticommunism was so broad and deep that failure to eject the Communists would probably have brought a Republican and conservative political triumph, followed by even harsher restraints on union activity and a full-scale assault on the New Deal legacy.

7

Partisanship and Anticommunism

THE PARTISAN USE of anticommunism by Republicans is obvious in the Hiss case and in others as well. Perhaps not as evident is the partisan element in the response to anticommunism by most active Democrats, particularly those in the Truman administration and Congress. The administration's policy toward Communists in government was a layered defense that made political though not logical sense.

The first layer was the assertion that in the 1930s and 1940s there had been no serious problem of Soviet espionage and no significant Communist presence in the government. Democratic spokesmen dismissed Republican charges as vicious partisan lies. President Truman, for instance, initially dismissed HUAC's hearings about Hiss as nothing more than Republican attempts to shift public attention from the failures of the Republican-controlled Congress.

As evidence against Hiss accumulated, however, dismissal was not possible, and the administration fell back to its second line of defense. Here it held that instances of Communists in government such as Hiss would be pursued, but that such matters were isolated. The Truman administration shifted its stance on Hiss, prosecuted him, and imprisoned him. Truman sanctioned the prosecution, but it was a reluctant conclusion. He regarded the Republican leaders of HUAC, particularly Nixon, as his deadly political enemies, and always hoped that information would turn up vindicating Hiss and discrediting Nixon.

The administration's third line of defense was that even though there had been no serious problem of Communist infiltration of the government, the government would nonetheless adopt stern measures to see that it did not happen again. In 1947 President Truman issued a sweeping executive order establishing a comprehensive security program for U.S. government employees, and in 1948 the Justice Department indicted CPUSA leaders under the 1940 Smith Act.

Anti-Communist liberals outside the Truman administration almost to a person quickly concluded that Hiss was guilty. This was a painful conclusion because of Hiss's identification with the New Deal and Republican use of the case to discredit the New Deal. Anti-Communist liberals were, however, more willing than most partisan Democrats to see the Hiss case as the symptom of a problem created by the Popular Front era of the late 1930s. To anti-Communist liberals, Hiss was an example of why the Popular Front alliance of liberals and Communists was misbegotten. Hiss was a double traitor; not only had he betrayed the United States, he had betrayed the New Deal and his liberal colleagues as well by using them as cover for his espionage. Thus Hiss was a product of the mistakes of the Popular Front wing of the New Deal, not of the New Deal itself, and the problem in any event was over. With the humiliating showing of Henry Wallace's Progressive party in 1948 and their expulsion from the CIO, Communists had ceased to play a significant role in the liberal movement. President Truman, molding a new Democratic foreign policy around containment of Soviet expansion, had become the first of a long line of cold war presidents.

While the newly minted cold war Democrats wished to close the book on the role of Communists in the New Deal era, Republicans were not so willing. In the face of assaults by Nixon and others, anti-Communist liberals had difficulty articulating a politically viable defense. Saying there had been a problem but it was now cleaned up was not a strong defense. This response left swing voters wondering why Democrats had a Communist problem in the first place and whether it really had been put right.

Many anti-Communist liberals dealt with the surfacing of Communists in New Deal institutions by portraying them as secret interlopers into the liberal movement. This conspiratorial portrait of communism allowed anti-Communist liberals to deny any ideological or political link between communism and the New Deal and to explain away exposures of Communist participation in liberalism. Anti-Communist liberals thus retroactively defined the New Deal. Their interpretation changed the history of the New Deal. Now Popular Front liberalism had not been a significant minority force in the broad New Deal but merely a tiny fringe movement whose influence was largely intellectual rather than organizational, limited to a few journals of opinion, some isolated radical enclaves in New York City and a few other places, and a handful of mavericks. This allowed anti-Communist liberals to protect the New Deal and its leader, particularly President Roosevelt, from any responsibility for the Communist presence in liberal institutions and the government. Post–World War II anti-Communist liberals were not inclined to see the ambiguous nature of the earlier Popular Front alliance or to understand how the fascist threat drove a segment of American liberals into a dubious embrace of Communists. Firm in their own cold war anticommunism, they could not or would not appreciate how the political context of the 1930s made it expedient for some New Deal leaders to tolerate and occasionally cooperate with the Popular Front.

This excessively conspiratorial view of the Communist problem provided a safe haven from Republican attacks by directing them away from Democrats and liberals and onto the Communist infiltrators. It allowed Democrats to join Republicans in designing a bipartisan solution to the Communist problem. Consequently, while liberals and Democrats opposed some of the measures that Republicans and conservatives proposed to meet the Communist conspiracy, they supported many or offered their own versions of others. In 1950, for example, Senate liberals proposed that the attorney general be authorized to detain potential subversives during a presidentially declared military emergency as an alternative to a more sweeping conservative measure. In

1954 Senate liberals, including Hubert Humphrey, proposed
outlawing the Communist party as an alternative to a conservative bill that denied National Labor Relations Act protection to
any union the attorney general judged to be Communist infiltrated.

Despite Republican hopes, the Hiss case failed to do serious
damage to the Truman administration in 1948; Truman won reelection and Democrats regained control of Congress. Whatever
the passivity of the Roosevelt administration and the early Truman administration toward Communists, Truman led the nation
into the cold war and reoriented American foreign policy around
the containment of Soviet expansion. Truman and the Democratic party were also largely freed of the Communist taint by the
withdrawal of Popular Front liberals into the Progressive party
and their support for Henry Wallace. In this context, 1948 Republican attempts to paint Truman and the Democrats as soft on
communism failed.

For Richard Nixon as an individual, however, it was different.
To Republicans, Nixon was a heroic figure who had simultaneously exposed a Soviet spy and given the Truman administration
a bloody nose. Nixon's political career soared. Even before the
Hiss case, Nixon scored a triumph in his 1948 reelection campaign. Because California law allowed candidates to file in the
primary elections of more than one party, Nixon filed in both the
Republican and Democratic primaries and won both. Having
defeated his Democratic opponent in the opponent's own primary, Nixon won an easy victory in the general election.

Once Hiss was convicted and Nixon's stand vindicated, Nixon
reached for higher office, running for the U.S. Senate in 1950.
He had an easy time of it. The California Democratic primary
was vituperative, ending with the incumbent U.S. Senator, Democrat Sheridan Downey, withdrawing. Representative Helen
Gahagan Douglas won but was badly scarred in the process.
Douglas (wife of movie star Melvyn Douglas) went into the campaign against Nixon knowing he might use the Communist issue
against her as he had against Voorhis. Douglas was no Popular
Front liberal and had spurned the Progressive party in 1948. But

she had refused to support President Truman's policy of providing military aid to Greece and Turkey. She had also denounced the House Un-American Activities Committee, the scene of Nixon's triumph against Hiss.

Then in June 1950 Communist forces from North Korea invaded South Korea. Even before the North Korean attack, Nixon had led the Republican assault on Truman's Asia policy for allowing mainland China to fall to Communist forces in 1949. When the North Korean attack caught American policymakers by surprise and American forces ill-prepared, Nixon's criticism of Truman's Asia policy looked prophetic.

With communism, foreign and domestic, looming as a major issue, Douglas opened her campaign against Nixon with a preemptive assault: she attacked Nixon as soft on communism and charged that on a series of measures before Congress he had voted with Representative Vito Marcantonio (American Labor Party, New York), the only ally of the Communist party in Congress. Douglas's gambit was a disaster in two ways. First, it had no credibility. Voters could not believe that the man who exposed Hiss as a Soviet spy, supported Truman's cold war initiatives in Europe, and called for sterner anti-Communist actions in Asia was also voting the way the Communists wanted. Second, the charge backfired. Douglas built her case by comparing a selection of Nixon's votes with those of Marcantonio. The Nixon campaign responded by distributing 500,000 copies of a comparison of *Douglas's* votes with those of Marcantonio. Neither comparison was fair, but since Douglas had started it, she had difficulty explaining why it was legitimate to compare Nixon's votes with Marcantonio's but not hers. Nixon followed up this pamphlet with a blizzard of brochures, flyers, and radio commercials depicting Douglas as soft on communism—domestic and foreign—and unwilling to confront the Soviets in the cold war. With American troops then in desperate battle against Communists in Korea, it was a devastating political attack, and Nixon won in a landslide.

In 1952 when Dwight D. Eisenhower, commander of Allied troops in Europe during World War II, won the Republican nomination for president, he chose Nixon as his vice-presidential running mate. Eisenhower was an immensely popular figure with a broad bipartisan, almost nonpartisan, appeal. Republicans, however, were only too aware that Dewey had lost his lead and the election in 1948 by taking too lofty an approach and not responding to Truman's highly partisan punches in the final months of the campaign. Nixon was picked to ensure this did not happen again; his role was to hit the Democrats just as savagely as he could while Eisenhower took an Olympian stance. Nixon was also chosen because of his reputation as an anti-Communist campaigner. Eisenhower did not wish to make domestic communism a central theme in his campaign, but he and other Republican leaders did hope to use it as a secondary issue. Thus Eisenhower made his centrist and moderate approach to government the motif of his campaigning while assigning anticommunism and other highly partisan and divisive issues to Nixon.

Nixon's theme, shared by many Republican campaigners in 1952, was "Corruption, Communism, and Korea." The first referred to the numerous scandals that marred the second Truman administration and the third to the administration having been caught flat-footed in Korea and then achieving no more than a bloody stalemate along the 38th parallel. The Communist issue was, of course, a natural for Nixon. He pounded away at the record of Roosevelt and Truman administration laxity toward domestic Communism as a security problem. The Hiss case still had a major public presence, and the actions of two prominent Democrats allowed Nixon to make full use of it. Dean Acheson, who became secretary of state in Truman's second term, had been a friend and colleague of Hiss at the State Department, and publicly continued to support Hiss even after he was convicted. To some, Acheson's remarks were a noble statement of friendship. To most Americans, the statement was inexplicable; Hiss, after all, had deceived and betrayed his friends, the Democratic party, the New Deal, and President Roosevelt as well as his country. Adlai Stevenson, the Democratic presidential nominee in 1952, had also provided Hiss's lawyers with a deposition supporting Hiss's character.

These acts allowed Nixon to savage the Truman administration and the Stevenson candidacy for naiveté and neglect of domestic communism and, in Nixon's harsher moments, for complicity in treason. Nixon, for example, called Stevenson, Acheson, and Truman "traitors to the high principles in which many of the nation's Democrats believe." Literally the phrase accused the three of betraying only certain political principles, not of betraying the nation, but in rhetorical context the use of "traitors" had stronger implications. Democrats, of course, regarded Nixon's charges as dishonest and beyond the bounds of acceptability, but they were no more dishonest than those used by Democrats in the early 1940s implicating Republicans in pro-Nazi treason. Eisenhower won the election with a massive majority, and Richard Nixon became vice-president of the United States.

While Nixon was the most successful Republican anti-Communist, Joseph McCarthy was the most notorious. McCarthy grew up on a Wisconsin farm, dropped out of school to work, then reentered to finish high school. He worked his way through college during the depression, became a lawyer, and dabbled in politics. In 1939 McCarthy won election to a circuit judgeship, defeating a longtime incumbent. After America entered World War II he joined the marines and served with the ground staff of the marines' air arm in the Pacific.

McCarthy had entered politics as a New Deal Democrat but later shifted to the Republican party. After his discharge from the marines, he entered the Republican primary for the U.S. Senate in 1946. There he faced a formidable foe, incumbent Senator Robert La Follette, Jr., member of a family that had long dominated Wisconsin politics. Robert Jr. entered the U.S. Senate after his father's death in 1925 and in the 1930s left the Republican party to found the Wisconsin Progressive party. In Washington he was a firm ally of Roosevelt's New Deal and one of the most highly regarded liberal senators. The New Deal, however, attracted too many of the Wisconsin Progressives to the Democratic party, and by the end of World War II the party expired.

Senator La Follette, ignoring invitations from the Democrats, attempted to win renomination as a Republican. But the Wisconsin Republican party to which La Follette returned was far more conservative than the one he had left. McCarthy, aided by his status as a young war veteran and by the conservative tide in 1946, defeated La Follette in the primary and overwhelmed the Democratic nominee in the general election.

McCarthy did not use the Communist issue in his primary campaign against La Follette. The senator had never suffered from Popular Front illusions about Communists and even in the 1930s had worked hard to keep Communists out of his Progressive party. McCarthy did raise the issue in the general election against the Democrats, but only as a lesser of several campaign themes. Once in the Senate, the attention McCarthy gave to the issue of anticommunism was unexceptional among Republicans, certainly nothing like Nixon's use of the Hiss case to make himself into a national figure. It was a Democratic attempt to give McCarthy a political black eye over a partisan speech in 1950 that caused McCarthy to stumble into the issue and made him a national figure.

In a routine Lincoln Day talk to a Republican women's club in Wheeling, West Virginia, McCarthy hit the Truman administration and the Democrats from a number of angles, but only one part of his speech received much press coverage. McCarthy criticized the Democrats for laxity in security matters (the Hiss case was then in the news) but also for allowing China to fall to the Communists. McCarthy implied that State Department reluctance to aid Chiang Kai-shek was due to the presence of concealed Communists in the State Department, and that State Department officials had failed to remove them. At one point McCarthy dramatized his point by saying, "I have here in my hand a list of 205—a list of names that were known to the Secretary of State as being members of the Communist Party and who nevertheless are still working and shaping the policy of the State Department." McCarthy had no list. There *was* a source for the figure 205, but it meant less than McCarthy stated. In 1946 Secretary of State James Byrnes had told Congress that a security screening of 3,000 department employees had cleared all but 284, and that of the latter group 79 had been discharged, leaving 205. McCarthy had no idea what had happened to the 205 since that time. For that matter, of the 284 only a few were not cleared because of possible Communist links; most were security risks because of factors such as alcoholism, financial irresponsibility, and criminal records. Even most of those with possible Communist links turned out to have entirely innocent associations. Thus there was no list of 205 Communists in the State Department; McCarthy was bluffing for rhetorical effect.

But a string of espionage cases and the rapid expansion of Soviet communism after World War II had made the Truman administration vulnerable on the issue, and McCarthy's charge was one of many such stings Republicans had been delivering. Democrats knew McCarthy was lying with his claim to have a list. They thought they could humiliate him and take some of the momentum out of the Republican attack by calling his bluff. The Democratic majority in the Senate appointed a committee under Senator Millard Tydings (Democrat, Maryland) to investigate the McCarthy charges. Democrats expected to show that McCarthy had no list and force him into a humiliating retreat. Democrats on the Tydings Committee saw their task as a political one and acted in a partisan manner. Tydings repeatedly interrupted McCarthy's opening statement of his case in order to prevent him from presenting a coherent defense. The hearings were disorderly, and the majority Democrats harassed and badgered witnesses favorable to McCarthy while those critical of McCarthy were given deferential and respectful treatment. As expected, the committee concluded with a vindication of the Truman administration's security policies.

The outcome, however, was not a humiliation of McCarthy but his political success. Democrats had responded to McCarthy's rhetorical attack not with rhetoric of their own but by using their Senate majority to give their partisan response the cloak of an official senatorial investigation and rebuttal. It was typical hardball politics, but McCarthy turned out to be much better at it than the

Democrats. He refused to retreat. Instead he threw up new numbers and reformulated his statement to cover up the fact that he did not have a list of 205 names. Relentlessly he took the offensive, stressing the failure of the Truman administration to halt Communist expansion in Asia; rehashing the *Amerasia* case, where the Truman administration had transparently engaged in a whitewash; and linking this to other lapses in internal security policies (some real, some not). McCarthy didn't prove his case, but he didn't have to. The Truman administration was on the defensive on these issues, and in this sort of political exchange McCarthy had only to make a plausible case.

In his original speech McCarthy had not named any of the 205, and the individuals he did name were normal political targets such as Dean Acheson, Truman's secretary of state. Democrats had not expected McCarthy to go below such accepted political targets by naming actual State Department employees. But McCarthy had the ethics of a street brawler and had no intention of playing the game by rules that allowed Democrats to win. He named names, though not very many, and often exaggerated evidence and used innuendo to conflate past sympathy for communism (in a few cases) or Popular Front liberalism (more often) or innocuous associations with insinuations of current treason. Among those he named were obviously strong allies of the Communist party who were not employees of the State Department; this confused the situation—probably McCarthy's intent. By the time Democrats were able to show that someone McCarthy named might have been a Communist but was never a State Department employee and couldn't have been on McCarthy's list, public attention had moved on.

The Tydings Committee not only failed to put down McCarthy, it brought him so much publicity that he became identified as a leading anti-Communist, a remarkable status for the senator given his lack of knowledge on the subject. Even several years later, after he had made himself into the nation's most identifiable anti-Communist, McCarthy's understanding of communism remained primitive: a jumble of ill-digested truths, half-truths, myths, and flat-out lies.

Several circumstances conspired to give McCarthy celebrity status. He was, above all, newsworthy because he was outrageous. He generated press coverage by his willingness to make irresponsible, lurid, and sometimes bizarre charges. At various times he implicated President Truman, Secretary of State Acheson, Secretary of Defense George Marshall, half a dozen professional American diplomats, and several high-ranking army officers in treason. Usually the treasonous charge was worded so that if pressed McCarthy could disavow it, but the implication and innuendo were clearly there. Even those who did not believe the specifics of McCarthy's charges felt that something had gone badly wrong with America's Asia policy and were upset over the stream of revelations about Soviet espionage and concealed Communists in positions of trust in their government. The Truman administration by the early 1950s had little credibility left on these issues.

McCarthy functioned as a partisan Republican bludgeon throughout 1951 and 1952, flailing away at the Truman administration's reputation. His exaggerated charges were wildly popular with partisan Republican audiences, particularly with the old isolationist right wing that thirsted for "pay back" for the years of torment they had suffered when New Deal liberals had taunted them as pro-Nazi and fascist. If McCarthy had confined his charges, however vicious, to those such as Marshall, Acheson, and Truman, all figures capable of defending themselves and striking back in the heat of political battle, he would have remained, as Nixon did, within the bounds of partisan politics. But McCarthy also brought into the line of fire people who were not part of the political arena; he was careless and indifferent about evidence; and he did not care if some of those he forced into the limelight were innocent. McCarthy's tactics were irresponsible, but like so much else in the anti-Communist era, they had their precedent in the antifascism of the 1930s. Recall that Representative Samuel Dickstein, who had led the congressional attack on domestic fascism, often published in the *Congressional Record* lists of people he regarded as fascists and Nazis. When one congressman complained that six people Dickstein had named as

Nazis swore they were not, Dickstein replied, "If out of these hundreds of names that I have buttonholed as fascists and Nazis or whatever I have called them, only six filed a protest, I think I have done a pretty good job."

Some of those McCarthy implicated in treacherous conduct were diplomats. These professional foreign service officers were forbidden an active role in political debate and could not reply in kind to McCarthy's charge that their policy advice about China had been motivated by nefarious links to Soviet communism. In these accusations McCarthy played the role of a political bully, viciously kicking individuals who could not defend themselves. One such was John Carter Vincent, one of the State Department's few Chinese specialists in the 1930s and 1940s, who had been an influential adviser on U.S. Asian policy. His attitude toward the Chinese Communists was naively optimistic, seeing them as the only hope for a better China, while his judgment of the nationalist regime of Chiang Kai-shek was harsh and pessimistic. From the perspective of the 1990s Vincent's judgments seem poor; but there was never any evidence that his views were motivated by secret Communist sympathies or by links to clandestine Communist activities. McCarthy and his allies, however, repeatedly hinted, suggested, and implied that Vincent was part of a cabal of Communists within the State Department that had manipulated American foreign policy to bring about the fall of mainland China to the Communists. Because of his status as a professional diplomat, Vincent could not reply to McCarthy's assaults. He was repeatedly investigated for disloyalty, and each of the investigations found no evidence of disloyalty or anything to suggest a security risk. But after John Foster Dulles became Secretary of State, he forced Vincent's resignation.

Another person brought into the limelight by McCarthy was Owen Lattimore. If the Hiss case was the greatest success among congressional investigations of American communism, the Lattimore case was one of the worst. McCarthy told the Tydings Committee and the Senate that Lattimore was "the top Russian spy," "one of the top espionage agents," the "chief Soviet espionage agent in the United States," and predicted that when the

Lattimore case was exposed "it will be the biggest espionage case in the history of the country."

Lattimore was a pioneering scholar of the little-known cultures of the Chinese borderlands of Mongolia, Manchuria, and the Turkic-speaking regions of inner Asia. In 1941 Generalissimo Chiang Kai-shek, leader of the Nationalist Chinese government, requested that the United States recommend a political adviser to assist his relations with the United States during the war against Japan. The White House, on the advice of Lauchlin Currie, recommended Owen Lattimore, and he served in Chiang's headquarters at Chungking during 1941 and 1942. Lattimore later served as deputy director of Pacific operations for the Office of War Information. In 1950 he was director of the School of International Relations at Johns Hopkins University.

McCarthy's charges were explosive, promising a new Hiss case. But right away there were problems with the case against Lattimore. Lattimore had never been an official in the State Department, the ostensible place at which the espionage had taken place, though he had worked with the State Department on various projects and at various times was associated with American diplomats. McCarthy flung a lot of rhetoric at Lattimore, with vague charges that he had "access to all the files" at the State Department and "comes in whenever he cares to," but the senator had no evidence of specific acts of espionage. McCarthy, indeed, had no case that Owen Lattimore had engaged in espionage and only weak evidence that he was a concealed Communist. Louis Budenz, a former *Daily Worker* editor, testified that a high party official had told him to regard Lattimore's pronouncements about Asia as those of a Communist. Budenz, however, had no direct knowledge of Lattimore's Communist allegiance, and even this indirect evidence was weakened by Budenz's circumstances. He had defected from the CPUSA in 1945, had been interviewed extensively by the FBI, and had written a great deal about his activities in the party and of what he knew or had heard of the party's underground work. But he had never mentioned Lattimore until 1950. This delayed recollection undercut the credibility of what was, in any case, secondhand evidence.

As the weakness of his case against Lattimore became clear, McCarthy altered the charge. In a rare half-retreat he now told the Senate, "I may have perhaps placed too much stress on the question of whether or not he had been an espionage agent." He went on to attack Lattimore as having inspired an Asia policy that allowed the Communists to take control of China. But McCarthy did not really care if he proved that Lattimore was a spy, because his objective was not Lattimore or even Soviet spies. McCarthy's chief target was the Truman administration in particular and New Deal liberalism in general; the Communist issue was the means to an end.

Lattimore testified at length to the Tydings Committee, denying repeatedly that he was a spy, had ever been a spy, was or had ever been a Communist, had any sympathy for communism, or had had any role in setting America's China policy. The Tydings Committee exonerated him, but his troubles were far from over. Senator Pat McCarran, a conservative Democrat from Nevada, shared McCarthy's view that Lattimore was a Soviet agent. McCarran, unlike McCarthy, wanted to expose Lattimore, not just use him to scar the Truman and Roosevelt administrations. McCarran headed the Senate Judiciary Committee's Internal Security Subcommittee, the Senate equivalent of HUAC and generally known as the Senate Internal Security Subcommittee (SISS). McCarran ordered a full-scale investigation of Lattimore and set out to prove that a cabal of concealed Communists in the government had manipulated America's China policy.

Where the Tydings Committee had been deferential to Lattimore, McCarran's committee was hostile. McCarran subjected Lattimore to twelve days of testimony and examination, constantly interrupted him, made gratuitous rude comments about his testimony, and sometimes asked him questions of such complexity and vagueness as to make an adequate reply impossible. Lattimore responded with equal hostility and rudeness. His answers were often evasive and his tone sneering, and he had convenient lapses of memory on key points of his record. McCarran, despite his single-minded effort and his command of ample investigative staff, could turn up no evidence that Lattimore had committed espionage or that he was a concealed Communist. He did, however, reveal that Lattimore's views about communism and the Soviet Union were such that most Americans would not want him anywhere near the making of American foreign policy.

The record showed that Lattimore had vigorously defended Stalin's grotesque Moscow Trials and had called the Soviet Union a democracy during the worst years of Stalin's dictatorship. During the period of the Nazi-Soviet pact he had taken the view that there was little to choose between Great Britain and Nazi Germany, had been a close associate of several of those who stole government documents in the *Amerasia* case, and had himself been on *Amerasia*'s editorial board for several years. Investigators also uncovered in the Institute for Pacific Relations files a 1938 letter in which Lattimore told a colleague that the Institute needed to lag behind the public position of the Chinese Communists "far enough not to be covered by the same label—but enough ahead of the active Chinese liberals to be noticeable," and should back the Soviet Union's "international policy in general but without using their slogans and above all without giving them or anybody else an impression of subservience." Nor did Lattimore later change his views; in 1949, just before the Communist invasion of South Korea, he said he wanted "to let South Korea fall—but not to let it look as though we pushed it."

None of this proved that Lattimore was a spy or even that he was a concealed Communist. The FBI, which did its own investigation, concluded that although Lattimore was pro-Communist in his sympathies, there was no reliable evidence that he was a Soviet agent or even a secret member of the CPUSA. But Senator McCarran was not satisfied to show that Lattimore held pro-Soviet views. He was sure that Lattimore was a major Soviet spy and insisted that the Justice Department find something in the twelve days of testimony before SISS that could be the basis for a perjury charge. Because McCarran was a powerful Democratic senator, Truman's attorney general responded. After the Justice Department's regular prosecutors balked at seeking an indictment, the attorney general brought in Roy Cohn, a hard-driving, win-at-any-price attorney, to handle the case. Cohn won a seven-count indictment for perjury. Some of the counts were based on Lattimore's incorrect testimony, but the substance was minor, the incidents old, and nothing more than poor memory may have been involved. Other points had more import but were not overt acts but rather states of mind or matters of opinion inherently difficult to prove or disprove in court. For example, the indictment charged that Lattimore lied when he denied knowing that certain authors whose articles he published in *Pacific Affairs* were Communists and that he had lied when he denied being sympathetic to communism. Federal courts twice rejected the indictments as involving states of mind and judgments that did not lend themselves to judicial determination in a criminal case. The Justice Department eventually dropped the matter. Although Lattimore was victorious in fighting the perjury charges with their implication of espionage, the revelations of his past sympathy for Soviet policies disqualified him for faculty status in programs training Americans for U.S. government foreign service. He left Johns Hopkins and spent most of his remaining academic career at the University of Leeds in the United Kingdom.

During the 1952 presidential campaign McCarthy served two roles. His exaggerated charges scarred the Democrats by attributing to the entire party the sins of its by-then-dead Popular Front wing. His greatest use, however, was in propitiating the Republican old right. This wing of the party was not happy with the moderate conservatism and mild style of Dwight Eisenhower, the party's presidential candidate. McCarthy's fire-breathing calls for hunting down and exposing those who had betrayed the nation (a group that included the leaders of the Democratic party in McCarthy's more perfervid speeches) expressed the old right's angry desire for revenge on liberals for what they themselves had endured during twenty years of Democratic presidents.

In 1953, when Eisenhower became president and Republicans took control of Congress, Republican leaders expected McCarthy to tone down his rhetoric. Republicans were now in a position to correct whatever internal security problems existed within the government, so McCarthy's charges no longer served any partisan purpose. He was pointedly not given a position on the Senate Internal Security Subcommittee, which had jurisdiction over matters involving domestic communism, because of concern about his irresponsibility. Instead he was awarded the chairmanship of the Governmental Operations Committee, a body that normally oversaw the efficiency of executive branch agencies.

It would take Republican leaders a year to realize it, but McCarthy had become uncontrollable. He reveled in the publicity and attention that his charges had brought to him. Hardly a week passed without one of his heated statements appearing on the front page of a major newspaper or being the subject of an editorial, an opinion column, or a television or radio broadcast. Not all or even most of the publicity was favorable. From the beginning, McCarthy faced harsh press attacks by leading newspapers. Intoxicated by notoriety, however, McCarthy enjoyed bad publicity almost as much as good.

Another type of intoxication fed McCarthy's increasingly reckless course. He had long been a heavy drinker, and part of his image was that of the hard-drinking, hard-fighting, macho ex-marine. By 1953 his drinking had turned into alcoholism, and his impressive physical frame had begun to deteriorate while psychologically he became increasingly erratic and irresponsible.

McCarthy's worst habits were exacerbated by his unfortunate choice for a top aide. McCarthy actually knew very little about the American Communist movement. Hoping to add some substance to his attacks, he employed Roy Cohn, Lattimore's prosecutor. Cohn was intellectually brilliant, prodigiously hardworking, and a highly effective litigator. He was also ruthless, given to breaking rules to get what he wanted, self-indulgent, and as avid a seeker of publicity as was McCarthy. Rather than restraining his superior, Cohn stoked his extremism and added his own large dash of irresponsibility. Although he always denied it, Cohn was homosexual (or bisexual) and eventually died of AIDS. Cohn's homosexual proclivities, closeted though they were, contributed to the final drama that destroyed McCarthy.

Before 1953 McCarthy's charges were part of an electoral

campaign against incumbent Democrats. With Republicans in charge of both the Congress and the presidency, beating up on Democrats lost much of its point and its publicity value. In order to sustain the attention he loved, McCarthy needed both to find new targets and to increase the vehemence and heat of his attacks. McCarthy's chairmanship of the Governmental Operations Committee provided him with the target: the U.S. government itself.

McCarthy made himself chairman of the investigative subcommittee of the Governmental Operations Committee. His committee had no jurisdiction over most matters involving domestic communism in general, but he could claim jurisdiction over Communist infiltration of government agencies. He could no longer target Democratic political appointees in the executive branch (they had all been replaced by Republicans), so his substitute targets were high-level civil servants, the government's permanent administrators. Initially they were an easier target for McCarthy than the Democrats had been because, as civil servants, they were not free to use the political arena to fight back. For that reason, McCarthy's attacks on civil servants moved him more firmly into the role of political bully. In the long run, however, the Eisenhower administration could not allow McCarthy to engage in disruptive forays into the executive branch. The senator's continued attacks would seriously damage the president's ability to govern.

McCarthy's first target was Eisenhower's nomination of Charles Bohlen, a career diplomat, as ambassador to Moscow. Within the professional foreign service Bohlen was regarded as one of its ablest members as well as one of its few Soviet experts; he had played a key role in converting Truman's cold war containment policy into a working diplomatic strategy. Years earlier he had attended the Yalta Conference, an event that symbolized Roosevelt's naiveté toward Stalin in Republican eyes. In McCarthy's view, Bohlen's mere presence at Yalta disqualified him to be ambassador to the Soviet Union. Typically, however, McCarthy did not attempt to prove that Bohlen had given Roosevelt bad advice or even that he had supported the Yalta agreement. Instead

McCarthy insinuated that Bohlen was a security risk and that the administration was hiding evidence of Bohlen's Communist links. It wasn't, and Eisenhower, though insisting on keeping the fight as low key as possible, refused to back down to McCarthy's demands that Bohlen's nomination be withdrawn. McCarthy led a floor fight against Bohlen in which he repeatedly implied, but did not outright assert, that Bohlen was a Communist sympathizer; McCarthy was crushed by a 74 to 13 vote to approve Bohlen.

The lopsided Senate rejection of his charges did not humble McCarthy. He went on to seek easier prey. He found it in the International Information Agency, the government's foreign propaganda arm and the successor to the World War II Office of War Information. Communists had infiltrated the agency during the war, but when it was reorganized in the late 1940s the Truman administration's personnel security program eliminated most of the Communist presence. The International Information Agency, however, was regarded with mistrust by many Republicans because of its origins as an emergency war agency independent of the regular federal personnel system, and because its staff was made up disproportionately of New Deal supporters.

McCarthy latched on to an internal agency dispute about where to site Voice of America transmitting antennae. He depicted the winning choice as an act of sabotage by pro-Communist agency officials who deliberately chose a poor site. Then he painted the agency's libraries in foreign countries as sources of Communist propaganda because they included books written by Communists or pro-Communists. Further, he defined as pro-Communist books written by liberal anti-Communists such as Arthur Schlesinger, Jr. In an attempt to appease McCarthy on something that it regarded as of minor importance, the Eisenhower administration pulled many of the books out of International Information Agency libraries, though most were quietly returned once McCarthy turned to other targets.

McCarthy's attacks on the International Information Agency damaged the agency's morale, diverted its leaders' time and attention, and seriously irritated the Eisenhower administration.

But McCarthy's hearings generated enormous press coverage, and he loved it. Roy Cohn orchestrated the attack and took a direct hand in a way that would eventually backfire on McCarthy. At Cohn's urging, McCarthy hired as an unsalaried "chief consultant" a young man named David Schine. Schine's only claim to knowledge about American communism was his authorship of a short pamphlet—unsophisticated and containing glaring errors, such as listing the wrong year for the overthrow of the Russian tsar. Schine himself was rich, handsome, and immature. While he did not share Roy Cohn's homosexual inclinations and there is no evidence of a relationship, there is no doubt that Cohn doted on him and treated the youth as a pampered pet.

With McCarthy's permission, Cohn took Schine on a governmentally financed tour of International Information Agency facilities in Europe. At stops in London, Paris, Bonn, Berlin, Athens, Rome, Munich, and Vienna, Cohn demanded that he and Schine be treated as government VIP's, and that International Information Agency officials be at their beck and call. Officials who denied his requests were publicly humiliated and threatened with firing. Nor was the tour a secret; Cohn loved publicity. He held frequent press conferences during the junket and reveled in demonstrating to the press that he had the power to intimidate government bureaucrats. For McCarthy the tour was a public relations disaster. The European press treated Cohn and Schine as jokes or as evidence that America was in the grip of a sinister demagogue. The American press treated the tour as an embarrassment for the United States. The tour emboldened McCarthy's critics to present him as a liability for American foreign policy.

The Cohn-Schine tour and young Schine's obvious unsuitability also allowed McCarthy's liberal critics to step up their whispering campaign that depicted McCarthy, Cohn, and Schine as closet homosexuals. McCarthy and Schine were not, and the insinuations were simply manufactured to discredit McCarthy. Cohn, on the other hand, was a hidden homosexual, though at the time perhaps a nonpracticing one. McCarthy was aware of the whispering campaign and was deeply indignant. But he had already set the standard by his own practice of insinuating that various liberal leaders and State Department officials were homosexual: Acheson was the butt of several McCarthy slurs about homosexuality. Nor was this the only tactic used by McCarthy that was now used against him. In his charges against government agencies, McCarthy used information surreptitiously supplied by employees whom he hailed as his "loyal American underground." McCarthy's critics were indignant about this, denouncing the practice as encouraging informing. But three sources—the Democratic National Committee, a prominent liberal critic of McCarthy, and the *Washington Post*—all thought they had developed a spy on McCarthy's own staff who was a disillusioned employee. The first two paid the informant directly while the *Post* promised to pay if the stories the newspaper planned to write on the basis of his information were syndicated. The informant, however, turned out to be a confidence man. He had never worked for McCarthy, and the documents and depositions he supplied about McCarthy's nefarious activities were fraudulent. A regular *Post* reporter, brought in to help in writing an exposure of McCarthy based on the informant's information, discovered the fraud and saved his paper from a major embarrassment.

In a more conventional and effective tactic, at the height of McCarthy's influence prominent liberals founded the National Committee for an Effective Congress, devoted entirely to bringing about the defeat of McCarthy and of congressmen like him. The Democratic Senate Campaign Committee also gave office space and staff support for the Clearing House, an informal anti-McCarthy central headquarters. The Clearing House sought to coordinate what had become a major effort by the Democratic party, the Americans for Democratic Action, most labor unions, and the National Committee for an Effective Congress to discredit the senator.

McCarthy ignored all the warning signs. After battering the International Information Agency, he turned on the army. This was a dangerous choice of target: the army had enormous prestige, and President Eisenhower was a proud professional soldier who had served with many of the officers who would shortly become McCarthy's victims. McCarthy's use of his subcommittee's investigatory powers to wage highly publicized forays into the army's internal affairs, and his public abuse of its officers, violated every standard President Eisenhower held for the appropriate relationship of the American military to its civilian superiors.

McCarthy's first military targets were laboratories in New Jersey that worked on radar and other electronic devices for the Army Signal Corps. McCarthy's hearings showed that security procedures at these labs at the end of World War II and for several years thereafter were sometimes careless. Some engineers employed by the labs had at one time associated with Communists and when questioned about it were evasive. It appeared to be another case where security procedures created in World War II to deal with Nazi espionage were not adjusted rapidly enough to deal with cold war threats. This suggested a need for review, but no evidence suggested that espionage had occurred. The Eisenhower administration and the army bureaucracy moved to appease McCarthy by hastily holding loyalty board reviews of several dozen laboratory employees. The accused employees were presented with a series of allegations and insinuations but were told they could not see the actual records and specifics of the allegations or even who had made them. Board members asked the employees questions about their religious beliefs, their attitude toward public versus private ownership of electric power companies, and their partisan voting habits. After the hearings more than half a dozen were fired. All brought legal actions against their firings and were later reinstated. In any case, McCarthy was not interested in a handful of engineers with backgrounds that might deserve a second look. By innuendo he implied that high-ranking military officials had been grossly incompetent or had deliberately allowed Communist penetration of the labs because of treasonous pro-Soviet sympathies.

McCarthy's next target was an army dentist named Irving Peress. Peress was a Communist, of that there was little doubt.

After finishing dental school he had been drafted, and like all draftees had filled out security forms. But the questions about belonging to various Communist organizations he had refused to answer. The clerks who processed his forms did not notice what he had done—a mistake, but not an uncommon one in as large a bureaucracy as the army. Peress was appointed an army dentist with the rank of captain.

McCarthy found out about Peress's Communist loyalties and opened a full-scale investigation of how a Communist obtained an army commission. To compound the army's embarrassment, Peress later had been automatically promoted and honorably discharged.

The Peress affair was a security error but a harmless one. Army dentists get little opportunity for espionage, and there is no evidence that Peress ever tried it. It should have been handled by the army internally. McCarthy's highly publicized hearings were only incidentally aimed at Peress. His targets were high-ranking military officers whom he accused of incompetence, even hinting of treason. McCarthy demanded courts-martial and criminal punishment of those connected with Peress's commissioning, promotion, and discharge, and in a monumental rage he denounced a veteran army general as not fit to wear the nation's uniform.

To that point the army had responded to McCarthy's public humiliation of its officers with only a limited defense, hoping that a combination of appeasement and patience would eventually lead the senator's attention elsewhere. McCarthy's attacks, however, had gone too far, and there was no prospect they would subside. President Eisenhower was furious at McCarthy's behavior but did not wish to respond personally to McCarthy's attacks; he realized that McCarthy thrived on publicity and would love to get into a public brawl with the White House. Rather, Eisenhower told the army not only to defend itself but to counterattack. The army did and brought about McCarthy's destruction.

The army went after McCarthy through Roy Cohn and David Schine. After his tour of Europe, Schine had been drafted. Cohn then used his position as McCarthy's aide to demand that the army grant Schine special privileges. In numerous meetings and phone calls to high-ranking officers, Cohn demanded that his young friend be given choice assignments, be relieved from tiresome duties usually given new soldiers, and receive frequent passes to visit Cohn. The requests were frequently accompanied with threats that Cohn would use his influence with McCarthy to ruin the careers of any officer who failed to meet Cohn's demands. While the army was attempting to appease McCarthy, it agreed to many of Cohn's demands. Once it shifted to a counterattack, it used the records it had kept to destroy McCarthy.

Since the start of mass conscription in World War II, most men had served in the armed forces. Few situations aroused public ire more than political pressure allowing some young men, particularly rich ones, preferential treatment in the military service. Cohn's abuse of his position to gain privileges for Schine was indefensible—but McCarthy defended it. He redoubled his attacks on the army and accused it of raising the issue of Cohn's conduct in order to sidetrack McCarthy's hunt for traitors in the army's higher ranks. By this time McCarthy no longer had a firm grip on reality and could not understand the basis of his public standing. Polls often showed him with a favorable public image, but that was chiefly because most citizens did not follow his actions closely and knew only from headlines that he exposed hidden Communists—a good thing in most people's minds. Defending special privileges for the drafted young friend of an aide was a different matter. This damaged McCarthy's standing with highly patriotic conservatives, hitherto a source of his support.

When Congress held a public investigation into the controversy, "Army-McCarthy" hearings were highly publicized, carried on television, and proved to be a disaster for the senator. Not only was his defense of Cohn's conduct an impossible task, but his physical and psychological deterioration had advanced considerably. Cohn himself realized the damage the hearings were doing and tried to get McCarthy to restrain himself, to no avail. To a huge television audience McCarthy looked ugly and mean, and his conduct appeared vicious and occasionally irrational. By then the press was largely hostile, and presented almost everything McCarthy did in a negative manner.

The Army-McCarthy hearings brought McCarthy's public standing so low that the Eisenhower administration and his liberal critics teamed up to finish him off. The Senate launched an investigation into McCarthy's conduct, particularly his rhetorical abuse of fellow senators and of military officials. In December 1954 the Senate voted 67 to 22 to censure McCarthy. The censure, and Democrats regaining control of the Senate in 1955, broke McCarthy's power. The press, which had aided his rise to national prominence by paying attention to his charges, now ignored him. His credibility was such that few persons in positions of authority any longer believed or cared about what he said. His charges no longer stung. His spirit broken, McCarthy's slide into alcoholism accelerated. In 1957 he died of cirrhosis of the liver at age forty-nine.

McCarthy's legacy was largely negative and nasty. His use of innuendo to accuse persons of espionage and sedition, his indifference to evidence or the accuracy of his charges, his bullying humiliation of weak opponents, and his device of insinuating that criticism of his tactics was evidence of Communist sympathies made civil discourse nearly impossible. The arbitrary quality of those he chose to denounce (the innocent, the guilty, and every gradation in between) spread fear widely within the ranks of government employees because there seemed to be so little logic to his targets. As a practical matter, McCarthy's investigations never directly affected more than a few hundred persons, but because of their capricious manner, *fear* of his investigations affected tens and perhaps hundreds of thousands of persons. Enormous media coverage of McCarthy also inspired hundreds of local imitators who used anticommunism in the same demagogic fashion and spread to other arenas the fear of arbitrarily being denounced as a Communist or as soft on communism. Again, the numbers of people directly affected were not large, but the numbers of those who feared that their employment, or a promotion, or simply their public standing might be threatened

by some junior-grade McCarthyist were probably in the hundreds of thousands.

By the late 1950s the ability of demagogues like McCarthy to
do real damage to innocent persons had passed. Only the remnants of the old Republican right and a few others continued to
look back on McCarthy as a fallen hero and on McCarthy's
methods as defensible. "McCarthyism" became a term of opprobrium, connoting mean-spirited fanaticism as well as false or
irresponsible accusation. Liberal anti-Communists had always
detested McCarthy, but most conservative anti-Communists also
came to regard him and his legacy as an embarrassment and a
mistake. Indeed, the negative consensus about McCarthyism became so well established that those seeking the historical rehabil-
itation of American Communists and Popular Front liberalism
have depicted all varieties of opposition to communism as forms
of McCarthyism.

8

Anticommunism at High Tide

VIRTUALLY ALL THE WEAPONS used against the threat of a fascist or Nazi fifth column in the late 1930s and early 1940s were used against the threat of Communist subversion in the late 1940s and 1950s. But the campaign against domestic communism was more sweeping because of the greater seriousness of the threat. America's domestic Nazis and fascists never enjoyed the membership, financing, organization, and institutional support (foreign and domestic) possessed by the CPUSA.

In 1948 the Truman administration, embarrassed by Republican use of its *Amerasia* cover-up and the exposure of Soviet espionage activities, shored up its anti-Communist credentials by indicting under the Smith Act twelve CPUSA leaders, including its chairman, William Foster, and its general secretary, Eugene Dennis. (Foster was in poor health, and prosecutors never brought him to trial.)

The Smith Act included a section on sedition that penalized those who advocated destruction of the government by force, or who took part in an organization that advocated such destruction. The Justice Department did not attempt to prove that the party engaged in overt revolutionary acts; rather it maintained that the systematic advocacy of the overthrow of the constitutional order through revolutionary Marxism-Leninism by itself constituted a crime under the Smith Act. For reasons of its own, the CPUSA decided not to offer a defense based on the First Amendment: to claim that no matter what the party advocated, it was speech protected by the Constitution. Instead Dennis and the other defendants claimed that since the 1930s the CPUSA had been a democratic socialist movement that adhered to a constitutional path to power. The government responded by showing that during this period the CPUSA, despite tactical shifts, had continued to use Leninist texts that supported violent revolution.

The atmosphere of the trial was raucous. By this time, in 1949, international tensions between the Soviet Union and the United States were extremely tense, even more so after the Soviets exploded an atomic bomb. Convinced that a Soviet-American war was imminent, American Communist leaders adopted confrontational tactics to publicize their view that the U.S. government was fascist in character. Both the defendants and their lawyers repeatedly interrupted the trial with verbal outbursts, berated witnesses, and shouted insults at prosecutors and the presiding judge, Harold Medina. Judge Medina jailed two of the defendants for contempt during the trial and, when the proceedings ended, briefly jailed all five defense attorneys for contemptuous conduct.

On a key point of law in the case, Medina ruled for the government and held that advocacy unconnected to overt revolutionary or violent acts could be a crime if "there is a sufficient danger of a substantive evil [overthrow of the government]" to remove the advocacy from the realm of otherwise protected free speech. The jury convicted all eleven defendants. All except one were sentenced to five years' imprisonment. Robert Thompson, the exception, received only three years in deference to his record as a decorated combat soldier in World War II. With good behavior, all would be released after serving about half their sentences. After conviction, all eleven defendants appealed, and the case was not settled until June 4, 1951, when the Supreme Court upheld the convictions in the case known as *Dennis vs. U.S.*

American Communists were convinced that the final conflict between the Soviet Union and the United States was now upon them and prepared for the apocalypse. The party had required all its members to "reregister," that is, to reapply for membership. This allowed the sloughing off of about a third of its members who were judged too weak to face what was expected to be a long night of fascist repression. When the Supreme Court announced its decision in *Dennis vs. U.S.*, the CPUSA divided itself into four layers under a plan originally devised in 1947.

The first layer was the open party organization under William Foster, with about seventeen thousand members. Communists expected this body to be declared illegal and its members arrested or scattered. Below the open party was a layer of several hundred "operative but unavailable" party cadre. These cadre dropped out of sight, changed their names, changed their jobs, and usually moved to a different region of the country. This second layer linked the open party to the third stratum, a layer of leaders and cadre designated as the infrastructure of an underground party that would take over once the open party was destroyed. This third layer also changed locations, names, and jobs. Finally, a small group of key cadre were sent outside the United States for safekeeping. This final group consisted mostly of younger leaders judged to be capable of rebuilding the party if both the open and underground organizations were destroyed.

Five of the *Dennis* defendants, including Eugene Dennis himself, were designated for the underground. All the *Dennis* defendants had been out on bond since their arrest in 1948. When the Supreme Court affirmed their convictions, four jumped bail and fled. Dennis intended to flee to the underground as well, but had the bad luck of being in jail serving a short-term conviction for contempt of Congress when his appeal was rejected. He went straight to prison.

The four who evaded prison were Henry Winston (organizational secretary), Gus Hall (Dennis's heir apparent), Gil Green (leader of the Illinois party), and Robert Thompson (leader of the New York party). With good behavior, Thompson would have faced only a year and a half in prison under his Smith Act conviction. But he feared that an American-Soviet war or a full-fledged fascist dictatorship was at hand and persuaded CPUSA leaders to send him into the underground in case he was needed to lead guerrilla forces against the American government. (Thompson had commanded a Communist battalion in the

Spanish Civil War and had served in the American army in World War II.) The FBI, however, caught up with Thompson and arrested him in a California mountain hideout in 1953. Four other underground Communists captured with him were imprisoned for harboring a fugitive. Thompson then had to serve his original sentence plus additional time for jumping bail. After his capture, Thompson was nearly killed when a fellow prisoner, an anti-Communist Yugoslav awaiting deportation, beat him with a lead pipe. Gus Hall was also caught while attempting to flee to the Soviet Union through Mexico.

After the Supreme Court upheld the *Dennis* decision in 1951, prosecutors indicted more than a hundred other CPUSA officials in what were known as the "second-string" trials. While several of these trials resembled the *Dennis* case, some of the defendants shifted their defense to one of free speech and avoided courtroom confrontation. In a number of these cases the presiding judges also expressed their discomfort with the standard used in the *Dennis* decision to distinguish between constitutionally protected and unprotected speech. In several cases trial judges directed acquittals or appellate courts voided convictions on procedural grounds.

The Supreme Court also had second thoughts and in 1957 retreated from *Dennis* by voiding the Smith Act conviction of California Communist leaders in the *Yates* case; revolutionary advocacy by itself was no longer sufficient for conviction. After *Yates vs. U.S.*, courts dismissed many indictments of Communists. By the late 1950s the Smith Act was no longer effective against the Communist party. Fewer than half of those convicted under the act went to prison, and most served relatively short sentences. A few states also prosecuted Communists under state sedition statutes or old criminal syndicalism laws. These state prosecutions sent a few Communists to prison, but in 1956 the Supreme Court in *Nelson vs. Pennsylvania* ruled that the federal government had preempted sedition cases, and thus effectively nullified most state prosecution.

State authorities did deliver a serious blow to the Communist party through their regulation of insurance companies. The International Workers Order, a Communist-run fraternal insurance company, provided the party with institutional and financial support made possible by a substantial insurance business among immigrant groups. State insurance regulators, spearheaded by New York, destroyed the International Workers Order by forcing liquidation of its insurance programs. Like so much else, this too had a precedent in the antifascist era in the federal government's seizure of a fraternal insurance company with links to immigrant Ukrainian fascists. In another act with an antifascist precedent, federal and state authorities moved against the Civil Rights Congress, the Communist party's civil liberties front group. Several of its leaders were jailed for contempt for refusing court orders to produce lists of its contributors. Among those jailed were Dashiell Hammett, a well-known writer (author of *The Maltese Falcon*), and Frederick Field of *Amerasia*. In the 1930s Congress's Campaign Expenditures Investigation Committee had exposed the financial backers of profascist organizations by issuing subpoenas for and publishing their financial records. When Joseph Kemp, an extremist who denounced the CIO as a Jewish Communist plot, refused to turn over lists of contributors to his organization, the committee had him jailed for contempt.

While the Smith Act did some damage to the Communist party by jailing several score of its cadre, the major anti-Communist laws passed by Congress never worked as they were intended. In 1950 Congress passed the Internal Security Act of 1950, better known as the McCarran Act. President Truman thought the bill's provisions were unneeded and excessive, and he vetoed it. But with anti-Communist sentiment aroused by the advent of the Korean War and Truman's standing near rock-bottom, Congress was in no mood to listen and overrode the veto. Congress later expanded and revised sections of the McCarran Act in the Communist Control Act of 1954.

The McCarran Act did not outlaw the Communist party. Instead it drew on ideas that Richard Nixon had proposed in 1947 by setting up an administrative mechanism to subject the Communist movement to systematic exposure. The bill created a gov-

ernment agency, the Subversive Activities Control Board, which
upon petition from the attorney general and after public hearings on the evidence could determine that an organization was
Communist dominated. Once done, the organization was
obliged to register with the Subversive Activities Control Board,
provide information about its officers, membership, and financing, and label its publications with its status. The assumption was
that although Communists would be allowed to continue their
activities, they could no longer do so covertly through front
groups. Thus as a practical matter they would be unable to operate successfully. This act too had anti-fascist precedents. New
York authorities had prosecuted an arm of the German-American Bund using a law requiring oath-bound organizations (the
law itself was the product of a nineteenth-century crackdown on
secret societies) to register with state authorities and provide
membership lists for public inspection. Other states also had laws
aimed at secret organizations, such as anti–Ku Klux Klan laws
that struck at Klan secrecy by criminalizing parades in Klan re-
galia that hid the Klansmen's identity.

In a series of hearings, the Subversive Activities Control Board
placed on the record a great deal of evidence about covert Communist activity through various organizations that were nomi-
nally independent bodies but actually were covertly controlled by
the CPUSA. The McCarran Act's formal exposure requirements,
however, never took effect. The CPUSA and its various fronts contested their registrations and undertook a protracted legal battle.
In 1964 the Supreme Court enervated the Subversive Activities
Control Board by holding that no party official could be required
to register the CPUSA because such an act would be coerced self-
incrimination that would place the person in jeopardy of the
Smith Act. In the end, neither the Communist party nor any
other organization registered with the Subversive Activities
Control Board. Because the Supreme Court had also eviscerated
the Smith Act, the federal judiciary effectively destroyed the
legal attack on the Communist party.

Another provision of the McCarran Act also proved to be a
dead letter. The act authorized the president to declare a national

security emergency and detain individuals considered to be potential saboteurs and spies. (The FBI had first prepared such a
list in the late 1930s, containing Nazi Bundists, fascists, and
Communists.) After the McCarran Act passed, specific plans for
detaining Communists and designated sites for detention camps
were prepared in case of war with the Soviet Union. But after the
Korean War ended and Stalin died, the Eisenhower administration regarded the plans as unneeded. The government sold or
leased the sites for other uses. No detention camps were ever
built, and no one was ever detained under the McCarran Act.

Of greater real impact on American society than either the
Smith Act or the McCarran Act was the federal government's
personnel security program begun by President Truman in 1947.
It was designed to prevent the recurrence of the Communist infiltration of government in the late 1930s and 1940s and the resulting embarrassing sting of cases of Soviet espionage.

That there was a need for such a program was manifest, but
the security program Truman established and Eisenhower later
expanded was ill-designed and worked poorly. It muddled together two separate concerns, loyalty and risk. The loyalty issue
dealt with whether there were grounds to doubt a person's loyalty to the United States based on that person's ties to a foreign
government or to a political movement with such ties. The risk
issue concerned whether a loyal person might nonetheless be a
security risk because of personal characteristics such as alcoholism, drug abuse, mental instability, a history of criminal behavior, compulsive gambling, serious financial indebtedness, or
susceptibility to blackmail due to sexual irregularities or threats
against relatives in a hostile nation. These various characteristics
made it irresponsible to trust that person to keep secrets. (An alcoholic might be loyal, but it would be foolish to trust a chronic
drunk with the nation's secrets.) Most government employees
went through the security screening without difficulty. Only a
few thousand of the government's vast work force lost their jobs
under the program. A somewhat larger number of job applicants
were rejected under the security program before hiring. Of those
fired or not hired, most fell into the second category of loyal but

risky (alcoholism was the leading disqualifier), and only a few hundred were fired or rejected on loyalty grounds. Because the two concerns were mingled in the same program, however, people rejected simply on risk grounds were sometimes unfairly tainted with suspicions of disloyalty.

The use of sexual irregularities, both heterosexual and homosexual, as a flag for potential security risk was more than an example of a puritanical moral code. As motives for espionage, sexual blackmail was a close competitor to ideology and money. In espionage parlance, the "honey trap" was a tried and true way of recruiting a source. The target, someone with access to sensitive material, would be lured into a sexual relationship, either homosexual or heterosexual. The sex act would be secretly photographed and the target then informed that unless he or she cooperated by carrying out espionage missions, the incriminating photographs would be sent to spouse, family, friends, employers, newspapers, and so forth.

But homosexuality as a security risk criterion in itself was also subject to misuse. The argument for exclusion of homosexuals was that because of a pervasive public hostility, most homosexuals were closeted and vulnerable to blackmail by foreign intelligence agencies. While there was an obvious logic to this argument, it was also to a certain extent a self-created problem: the potential for a hostile intelligence agency to blackmail a closeted homosexual was reinforced by making homosexuality an offense that could be used for dismissal. Further, there is no doubt that at various times individual security officials conducted wide-ranging hunts for homosexuals that were far more expressive of loathing for homosexuality than of concern about security.

Procedures under the personnel security program were also poorly designed. The act established a series of loyalty boards that considered cases of adversely affected employees. But the procedures provided that in considering information about a government employee, the source of the information could be kept confidential from the employee. This made it difficult and often impossible for the employee to contest the credibility of the source and to rebut the allegation. The FBI, which furnished much of the information used by the loyalty boards, as a matter of policy refused to disclose its sources of information because it feared such disclosure would make it more difficult to gather new information. The result was that in some cases acquaintances and coworkers, under the cloak of anonymity and out of ignorance or viciousness, confused any type of unconventional behavior with disloyalty. Although this practice continued into the 1960s, eventually the use of concealed informant information in security screening was prohibited.

Some of the persons who served on the loyalty boards were incompetent or biased. Some board members thought a belief in mixing black and white blood in blood banks or failure to belong to a church were grounds for finding an employee a security risk. Alternately, some board members regarded it as impossible that any respectable-looking middle-class government employee could ever be a security risk.

The rapid expansion of the personnel security system in the early years of the Eisenhower administration brought in a corps of security officers who were ill-prepared for the job. Many of these posts were filled by retired FBI agents. The FBI was an investigative agency, and its agents were well trained to gather information while avoiding its evaluation. That task was left to the Justice Department's prosecutorial arm. The personnel security system, however, placed enormous evaluative, not just investigative, responsibilities on the security officer, and many officers proved incompetent for the task.

Remember that during the 1930s and early 1940s several hundred thousand Americans were briefly members of the CPUSA, most for less than two years. Even more Americans had been for some time members of one or another front group secretly manipulated by the party. While some of these former Communists maintained ideological sympathies for communism, many— probably most—did not. Sophisticated security officers were aware of this and regarded brief membership in the CPUSA or one of its fronts ten or fifteen years in the past as cause for an evaluation but scarcely proof of a security risk. Many former party members received security clearances after evaluations by skilled security officers. But many of the security officers hired during the rapid expansion of the program under Truman and, even more, under Eisenhower were unskilled in appraising ideological matters and oblivious to the difference between a brief and disenchanted party or front member and a hard-core Communist. As a consequence, thousands of cases were forwarded to loyalty boards based on unevaluated allegations that, once evaluated, vanished as inconsequential. Meanwhile the employees in question had been unnecessarily alarmed and their morale damaged, supervisors and coworkers might become mistrustful, chances for promotion or choice assignments reduced, and much time and effort wasted. In a sensible system, many of the cases sent to loyalty boards would never have reached that stage.

In a somewhat modified form, the personnel security program also extended to a number of privately owned companies doing sensitive defense work. Here too several thousand workers were discharged and others not hired on the grounds of potential security risk or, on rare occasions, disloyalty. The government was particularly sensitive about this area due to the Communist party's record of using its union cadre to promote labor unrest in order to disrupt weapons production during the period of the Nazi-Soviet pact. Maritime workers were subjected to the most severe security check. If war with the Soviet Union came, the government reasoned, the decisive battle would be fought in Europe, and the American military would largely depend on sea transport to reach the fighting front. The maritime area was also of concern because in the 1930s and 1940s Communists had made deep inroads in several maritime unions. The Coast Guard, which licensed maritime workers, excluded from merchant shipping several thousand seamen with suspect records, and the once strong Communist role became a memory. Only the West Coast longshoremen's union, a shore-based trade, retained a major Communist presence.

One prominent feature of the loyalty-security system was the "attorney general's list." This list originated in World War II when Attorney General Francis Biddle sent government security officers a list of more than forty profascist, pro-Nazi, or pro-

Japanese organizations. Membership in any of the organizations was regarded as possible evidence of disloyalty. In 1947 this list was updated by the Truman administration and later by the Eisenhower administration with scores of Communist party front groups and auxiliaries. For a decade, whether one was or had been a member of an organization on the attorney general's list was a standard question on federal government security forms as well as those of a few state governments and even a handful of private corporations. Later it was replaced by a more general question about membership in any organization advocating the overthrow of the government. (For some years the form also inquired about close relatives who belonged to organizations that advocated the violent overthrow of the U.S. government, a question that gave some Southerners with grandfathers who had served in the Confederate army pause to consider just how close was close.)

The mind-numbing clumsiness of the federal government's application of uniform regulations to diverse situations, present in so many areas of federal government activity, is nowhere better illustrated than in the extension of the personnel security system to the entire federal government, not just to sensitive areas. Although personnel security regulations allowed agencies to apply different levels of scrutiny to holders of sensitive and non-sensitive jobs, a pervasive desire to avoid criticism for loose security led to hundreds of thousands of nonsensitive jobs being defined as sensitive. This produced the incongruous situation wherein a government inspector checking meat sanitation in a remote rural county sometimes was subject to the same security scrutiny as a procurement official in a military supply agency dealing with munitions stocks. After a 1956 Supreme Court decision in *Cole vs. Young* (involving application of personnel security regulations to a food and drug inspector), courts required the government to differentiate better between security-sensitive jobs and others requiring less scrutiny.

Despite improvements, the system continued to require expensive background investigations of many people in jobs only marginally related to national security. The result was a costly

personnel security system that subjected many people to unnecessary investigations while failing to provide continuous coverage of those in highly sensitive positions. This system was unable
to prevent a number of egregious breaches of American security,
such as the case of Jack Dunlap, an army courier for the super-
secret National Security Agency (NSA) who in the late 1950s
stole large numbers of classified documents and sold them to the
Soviets; William Martin and Bernon Mitchell, two NSA cryptographers who secretly joined the CPUSA and defected to the Soviet Union in 1960; John Walker, Jr., a navy petty officer who for
more than fifteen years turned over massive amounts of military
secrets to the Soviet Union for money; and, most recently,
Aldrich Ames, a CIA officer who in the late 1980s and early
1990s destroyed much of the CIA's covert operations against the
Soviet Union by turning over to the KGB names of Soviets who
were assisting American intelligence. In each of these cases, in
retrospect, the traitors exhibited signs of their activity—free-
spending, lavish behavior in several cases—that early on would
have alerted personnel security officers had they been looking,
but they were not. One reason they were not is that from the
beginning, the bulk of the government's enormous personnel
security apparatus was devoted to routine investigations of
government officeholders with little real national security sensitivity.

The needlessly broad sweep of the government's personnel
security system was in large part due to partisan political considerations. The Truman administration implemented a broader-
than-needed system to protect its flank from Republican
criticism, while Eisenhower expanded it to justify Republican
criticism that the Truman program was too weak.

The political symbolism and partisan cynicism that lay behind
the structuring of the personnel security system was vividly illustrated in the first year of the Eisenhower administration. In
April 1953 Eisenhower issued a new personnel security order
greatly strengthening what Republicans said had been an ineffective Truman system. That fall the Eisenhower administration
announced the results of its new program: as a *New York Times*

headline put it, "U.S. Aide Reports 1,456 Reds Ousted." The notion that 1,456 persons had been forced out of government employment under the administration's personnel security program became a staple of Republican spokesmen, Eisenhower cabinet members, and the president himself. This massive purge of government employees seemed to justify the most heated Republican attacks on the Truman administration as soft on domestic communism. Historical treatment of this revelation has often accepted the purge as a fact but given it a reverse spin: the fifteen hundred fired are depicted as victims of McCarthyist paranoia, innocent government employees fired for unproven and trivial allegations of political nonconformity. In fact it appears there was no Eisenhower purge in 1953. In order to justify their campaign rhetoric, Eisenhower administration officials decided to claim that massive numbers of security risks had been eliminated from the government. But the new security program was still being set up and had not yet (and would not, even when fully functioning) identified and discharged very many security risks. To justify its rhetoric, administration officials reviewed the personnel files of everyone who had left government service in 1953. If in any file any allegation was found that might be construed as having security implications, the separation was deemed to have been the elimination of a security risk. Yet virtually all of the 1,456 cases were of people who had left government service for other than security-related reasons. To give one example, administration spokesmen attributed 110 discharges to the Department of Health, Education, and Welfare. A security officer in this department wrote in a memoir that the 110 were a tabulation of "the names and numbers of persons who had recently resigned, retired, been transferred, or died, and in whose files there had been some allegation or other derogatory information in order to support the claims of 'security risks removed.' "

Many, but not most, state and local governments also enacted personnel security requirements, though their enforcement was often lackadaisical or even nonexistent. More common was the requirement of public employees to sign loyalty oaths, sometimes oaths containing specific disavowals of communism, Nazism, and fascism. Some states attached loyalty oaths to trivial matters, such as New York's requirement for some years that persons wanting a fishing license sign a loyalty oath, or Indiana's requirement that professional wrestlers sign an oath. Where loyalty oaths were required, most people signed without hesitation, but some regarded this as an inappropriate questioning of their loyalty, an invasion of their private convictions, or a violation of their constitutional rights. Holding that positions of trust required candor, several states and some educational institutions also fired employees who took the Fifth Amendment when testifying about Communist activities. Court decisions on the legality of loyalty oaths were confused, with courts voiding some and upholding others depending on the wording, appeal procedures, and other circumstances.

A few private companies without government military contracts imposed loyalty requirements. Several professional organizations also passed loyalty oaths, and several bar associations took the position that Communist lawyers should be disbarred. Because private corporations and professional organizations had no investigatory power, the requirements were usually purely symbolic. There were, however, some cases of employees fired by private companies and lawyers disbarred when they were revealed as Communists by congressional hearings, court actions, and newspaper stories. On a number of occasions the FBI harassed concealed CPUSA cadre by informing their employers of Communist links, often resulting in their firing.

Ultimately the federal government's personnel security program affected about three million military personnel and civilian Defense Department employees, about two million other federal civilian employees, and three million to four and a half million civilian employees of defense industries. Loyalty oaths or some other security requirements also affected about two million state and local government employees. Add to this some private-sector loyalty policies, and a total of ten million to twelve million workers were affected when this system was at its peak. Although this includes much purely nominal enforcement in state and local governments and the less sensitive defense industries, this was a significant number of affected workers. The total, however, was still less than 20 percent of the work force, and strict scrutiny was applied to only about 10 percent. This left at least 80 percent of all jobs unaffected. During the anti-Communist era, some Communists faced employment difficulties. Several thousand Communists (some open but most concealed) lost their jobs in the affected sectors, some had professional careers disrupted, but virtually all found work elsewhere. Even Alger Hiss, after conviction, found employment as a stationery salesman.

In addition to loyalty oaths, several states enacted elaborate anti-Communist laws or sedition statutes. Maryland's Subversive Activities Act of 1949 was the most comprehensive. The Ober Law, as it was named after its author, was approved by a vote of 259,250 to 79,120 in a 1950 referendum of the state's voters. The law defined and banned all subversive organizations, gave state authorities the power to dissolve any organization found to be subversive, to seize its property and records, to fine anyone who continued membership in a banned organization $5,000 with a prison term of up to five years, and to fine anyone who continued as an officer $20,000 with up to twenty years in prison. On paper it was a drastic law. In practice, no organizations were ever banned, no property or records seized, and no one fined or imprisoned under the Ober Law. Maryland officials made no serious attempt to enforce the law, and after its passage the public that had massively endorsed it by referendum was indifferent to the lack of enforcement. The Ober Law's actual function was symbolic, that is, to show pervasive public disapproval of communism. The Communist party continued to function legally in Maryland, but the Ober Law hung over its head as a warning. Other examples of unenforced (and legally unenforceable) symbolic anti-Communist laws were those of several cities—Jacksonville, Florida, and McKeesport, Pennsylvania, for example—that banished Communists from living in the town.

Several state legislatures, notably in California, Illinois, and Washington, also launched investigations modeled on the Dies Committee or HUAC. One of the most active state investigations occurred in New York. In 1940 and 1941, during the Nazi-

Soviet pact, State Senator Frederic Coudert and Assemblyman Herbert Rapp chaired an investigation of New York City public colleges. Based on the testimony of disillusioned former party members, the Rapp-Coudert Committee called a number of Communist teachers to testify; most denied their membership. New York had had a teacher loyalty oath since 1934, and after the investigation, educational authorities forced about a dozen faculty members to resign and fired twenty others. The investigations did not establish that the instructors involved had engaged in propaganda in the classroom, though it was demonstrated that the party maintained secret caucuses of faculty. Most of those fired had lied about their Communist membership or refused to testify to the legislative investigators, so the discharges were often based on lying and concealment. One college instructor was jailed for perjury for lying under oath about his party activities.

But honesty about membership did not protect a Communist teacher. Authorities took the view that although membership in the Communist party was legal, the CPUSA espoused an antidemocratic ideology, thus membership was incompatible with the responsibilities of a teacher in a public institution. A sophisticated version of this position was advanced by the prominent philosopher Sidney Hook. Hook, who had been close to the Communist party in the early 1930s, in 1953 published *Heresy, Yes—Conspiracy, No!* in which he declared that schools ought not to discharge teachers for privately held political views, including Marxism-Leninism. But Hook viewed Communist party membership as a different matter. He argued that the CPUSA was not a philosophical advocacy group but a political conspiracy aimed at the destruction of American democracy and required its members to adopt specified attitudes toward matters of science, history, and literature. Consequently, Hook argued, Communist teachers were not prepared "to follow the truth of scholarship wherever it may lead" and were disqualified as teachers.

After the Rapp-Coudert hearings, New York authorities also turned to the city's public schools and fired or forced out several dozen more Communist teachers. New York City contained well over a third of the CPUSA's total membership and included a number of college faculty and school teachers. Of the city's roughly 35,000 public school teachers, somewhere between 500 and 1,000 were Communists. With this base, in the late 1930s Communists dominated the city's Teachers Union Local 5 which at that time had a membership of about 4,000. The Rapp-Coudert hearings and later investigations resulted in the discharge of only a fraction of the total number of Communist teachers, but it crippled their activity. Local 5, for example, in 1941 was expelled from its parent union, the American Federation of Teachers (AFL), after it refused to eliminate its Communist leadership. Under pressure from school authorities and isolated from the mainstream labor movement, it was later eclipsed by a rival non-Communist local sponsored by the American Federation of Teachers.

During the *Dennis* trial, the CPUSA was shocked when more than a dozen of its members testified against it. All were FBI informants, either disillusioned party members whom the FBI had cultivated or agents planted in the party by the Bureau. FBI director J. Edgar Hoover largely accepted the fifth-column paradigm. He tended to see the CPUSA as principally a covert-warfare agency that was engaged in espionage and prepared to act as an internal sabotage and disruptive force to aid the Soviet Union in time of war. The Bureau built up files on CPUSA clubs, its officials, and its various fronts. Bureau agents attended open party meetings, recorded speeches, gathered literature, tapped the phones of party activists, and kept records of the travels and meetings of party officials. On several occasions the FBI broke into party offices to plant listening devices or copy documents.

Most of the FBI informants were rank-and-file party members with little responsibility. A few held middle-level party positions. Several of the FBI's prized informants in the 1950s were engaged in the transfer and "laundering" of the generous Soviet financial subsidies without which the party might have withered into a tiny radical sect. In large part the FBI simply gathered information and built up files. From time to time some of the

evidence or a few of its informants would be produced by prosecutors in trials of Communists under the Smith Act, against
concealed Communist union officials who signed the anti-Communist oaths required by the Taft-Hartley Act, or in Subversive
Activities Control Board hearings. The files also functioned as
the basis for the removal from government employment of concealed Communists under the personnel security program.
Hoover also provided information to state and local authorities
that led to the firing of employees with ties to the Communist
party. Just as he had during the antifascist era, Hoover also
leaked FBI information to journalists. The resulting press stories
usually disrupted organizations or activities in which concealed
Communists were engaged.

On occasion Hoover authorized disruptions and the planting
of false information that led the CPUSA to make errors. In order
to disrupt the party's New York organization, its largest, agents
planted information suggesting that William Albertson, head of
the New York organization, was an FBI informant. He was not,
but party leaders were convinced by the FBI's faked evidence
and expelled him.

Just as in the antifascist era, a literature of exposure developed.
Many books by disillusioned former Communists appeared.
One energetic ex-Communist writer was Louis Budenz. A labor
activist in the 1920s, an early official of the American Civil Liberties Union, and close to the Socialist party, in the early 1930s
Budenz moved further left. He first joined the American Workers party led by the independent radical A. J. Muste; but
Muste's radicalism was insufficient for Budenz, and he moved to
the CPUSA. There Budenz rose quickly to membership on its
New York state committee, then on the national central committee, and in 1941 he became managing editor of the *Daily Worker*
and was on the fringe of the party's top leadership, even attend-
ing irregularly the meetings of the party's ruling political bureau.
In 1945, however, Budenz underwent a spiritual crisis, left the
CPUSA, and was received into the Roman Catholic church by
Bishop Sheen at Saint Patrick's Cathedral in New York. He

then joined the faculty of, first, Notre Dame and then Fordham University, writing, lecturing, and testifying widely about communism as a subversive threat. His first book was *This Is My Story*, a largely autobiographical 1947 work about his journey from revolutionary to Catholic. It was followed by *Men Without Faces: The Communist Conspiracy in the USA*, a 1950 book that presented a largely fifth-column interpretation of the CPUSA. His later writings included *The Techniques of Communism*, a 1954 book emphasizing the party's conspiratorial nature, and a 1966 book, *The Bolshevik Invasion of the West*, on the use of political subversion as a Soviet cold war strategy. Budenz's early testimony and writings were largely accurate, and some points that were questioned at the time have been confirmed by documents from Moscow's archives in recent years. For example, in 1950 Budenz identified an obscure mid-level CPUSA official, Rudy Baker, as having a role in the leadership of the party's underground. No academic scholars ever attributed such a role to Baker or gave any credence to Budenz's claim. But in 1995 newly available documents identified Baker as the head of the CPUSA underground from 1938 to the mid-1940s. In this case Budenz had been right and mainstream historians had been wrong. Budenz, however, sometimes exaggerated his direct knowledge, and some of his statements on matters about which he had earlier said nothing, such as his testimony on Owen Lattimore, are of questionable credibility.

The most famous of the ex-Communists, Whittaker Chambers, published *Witness*, a widely read account of his life as a spy. Chambers's book displayed considerable literary elegance and power, though many liberals found its philosophical rejection of the liberal worldview, religious subthemes, and dark apocalyptic overtones distasteful. Many of the FBI's informants inside the CPUSA produced books on their experiences. One of the most successful was Herbert Philbrick. Philbrick entered the CPUSA in 1944 but from the beginning was an FBI informant. He worked as a Communist activist in Massachusetts, leading a party branch consisting largely of professionals who concealed their party membership. He surfaced as a government witness in the *Dennis* case in 1949. After that he testified to congressional committees and as a prosecution witness in a number of legal assaults on the party. After he surfaced he wrote *I Led 3 Lives: Citizen, "Communist," Counterspy*, which sold well and was turned into a television series of the same name. The TV series was routine in quality and interjected much more melodrama into Philbrick's story than was ever found in his testimony or his book; it achieved a modest audience. Between his book, the television series, and lecture fees, Philbrick enjoyed a comfortable income. He provided accurate testimony in courts and before Congress and his book was a reliable account of what he observed as a low- to middle-level party activist. He also stayed close to the FBI, praised the Bureau's role, and accepted FBI advice about how far he should go in his public announcements. Hoover, in turn, promoted Philbrick as a reliable source.

While Chambers and Philbrick were at the reliable end of the continuum of exposure literature, Harvey Matusow was at the other. As a young man in his twenties, Matusow had joined the Communist party in 1947 in New York. In 1950 he contacted the FBI and became an informer, receiving about $70 a month in expense money. Early in 1951 the CPUSA identified him as an informer and expelled him. He immediately became a professional anti-Communist, receiving lecture fees and payments for magazine articles such as "Reds in Khaki," about Communists in the armed forces, for the *American Legion Magazine*. He testified as a prosecution witness in several trials of Communist party officials, and in his early testimony appears to have been largely accurate. But with time his testimony both in courts and even more so in his personal lecturing became more and more bizarre. He had not been in the CPUSA long, had never held a significant post in the party, and was unsophisticated. Perhaps to sustain his marketability as an anti-Communist lecturer or because he obviously enjoyed the media attention, he began to exaggerate and eventually to lie on a massive scale. His testimony about the party drifted toward a fifth-column stereotype, as with his claim that he had personal direct knowledge of the party's secret plans to sabotage American industry in time of war with the Soviet Union.

By 1954 Matusow had exhausted his standing as an ex-Communist: prosecutors had grown uneasy about his reliability as a witness, and the media increasingly ignored him. He then shifted from exposing Communists to exposing ex-Communists, including himself. In 1955 he published *False Witness* in which he announced that he had lied about many people he had identified as Communists. Matusow's turnabout came with the same strident tone he had used when he was denouncing the Red Menace, and he quickly became a professional "anti-anti-Communist," giving paid lectures on the evils of anti-Communism to left audiences. To complicate matters, the firm that published *False Witness* was headed by concealed Communists and allies of the party. In addition, party-led unions and party fronts promoted the book's sale. Was Matusow's new stance a repentance for past perjury, or did he seek only to regain media attention and a new market for lecturing? He had so mixed together truth, half-truths, and lies that sorting it out was a near impossibility. His confession of perjury tainted a number of trials in which he had been a witness; some cases were retried and others simply abandoned. An angry Justice Department indicted Matusow for perjury. Having announced his guilt in his book, Matusow had no real defense and was easily convicted and imprisoned.

Because dislike of communism was deep and broad among Americans, all sorts of groups with other agendas attempted to tie their programs to the anti-Communist cause. Educators used anticommunism and the cold war to justify greater school expenditures, arguing that an educated America was needed to defeat the Soviet Union in the cold war: the federal measure to aid education in the 1950s was thus oddly titled the National Defense Education Act. Supporters of what became the interstate highway system initially presented the program in the 1950s as a network of "defense highways" to speed the transport of troops and supplies.

Others used anticommunism as a weapon in their own polemical battles. Classical artists of the American Artists Professional

League denounced modern art as a subversive style promoted by pro-Communists. This issue produced one of the odd juxtapositions of the era: Stalin hated modern art, suppressed it in the Soviet Union, and allowed only classical styles and the propagandistic "socialist realism" to be used by Soviet artists. Meanwhile, modern art styles were highly popular among Western Europe's left-learning intellectuals. Both the State Department openly and the CIA covertly used modern art as a weapon in the cold war by promoting American modern art exhibitions and tours in Western Europe, thus contrasting the openness of American democracy to the suppression of the Communist bloc. Meanwhile Representative John Rankin, one of the most reactionary of anti-Communists, absurdly denounced the State Department's backing of modern art exhibitions as evidence that its officials were secretly pro-Communist.

Some critics of the new musical phenomenon of rock-and-roll indignantly denounced this new teenage music as part of a Communist plot to destroy the moral fiber of the nation's youth. One ex-Communist, Kenneth Goff, attached himself to the anti-Semitic demagogue Gerald L. K. Smith and promoted the notion that fluoridating drinking water, approved to prevent cavities, was a Communist plot. One fanatic attacked the popular children's story of Robin Hood as subliminal Communist propaganda because it glorified robbing from the rich and giving to the poor; another insisted that the Girl Scouts were subversive. While these and other bizarre charges occasionally produced localized consequences, overall they were ignored by most Americans. Modern art triumphed in America's professional art world, rock-and-roll dominated American popular music, most cities fluoridated their water supplies, the sale of Girl Scout cookies did not suffer, and Robin Hood and the Merry Men of Sherwood Forest remained as childhood heroes.

A variety of far-right organizations attempted to use anticommunism as a recruiting tool. The most famous was the John Birch Society, organized in the 1950s by Robert Welch, a wealthy Massachusetts candy manufacturer. There *was* a John Birch, but he had had nothing to do with the society that bore his name.

Birch had been a young American missionary in China when the Flying Tigers, a group of volunteer American combat pilots, were formed to help the Nationalist Chinese in their war against Japan. Birch became a chaplain and intelligence officer (he spoke Chinese) for the Tigers, who were later integrated into the American army. By war's end Birch was a captain. He was killed in northern China a few days after Japan surrendered when his reconnaissance unit ran into a hostile Chinese Communist guerrilla patrol. Welch treated Birch as the first victim of Communist aggression in World War III and named his society after him.

Welch and his organization took the view that since Franklin Roosevelt and the New Deal, the American government had been in the grip of a sinister collectivist conspiracy that was consciously and deliberately destroying American republican values and preparing for a total Communist takeover. Virtually everything the federal government did, from Social Security to the building of interstate highways, was seen as part of the Communist conspiracy. Paranoia and conspiracy were not simply part of the Birch society message but its all-consuming core. In his 1958 book *The Politician*, where he set out the principles that guided the John Birch Society, Welch wrote that President Eisenhower was "a dedicated, conscious agent of the Communist conspiracy," that the president's brother, Milton Eisenhower, a respected educator and former diplomat, was "actually Dwight Eisenhower's superior and boss within the Communist party," and that Secretary of State John Foster Dulles, a strident anti-Communist in reality, was "a Communist agent." These and other absurdities resulted in the John Birch Society's isolation from mainstream conservatism and consignment to the lunatic fringe of politics. The organization's membership was dedicated, though never large, and probably never exceeded five thousand.

One of the most determined tagalong campaigns was that of Southern racists in support of segregation. The movement for full legal equality for black Americans began to gather momentum in the late 1940s and became one of the nation's chief defining issues in the 1950s. Proponents of civil rights insisted that promotion of racial equality was not only compatible with

America's anti-Communist commitment but an asset in its cold war against Soviet communism. Southern segregationists, however, promoted the idea that integration was a Communist plot. The White Citizens Councils, a federation of Southern white racist organizations, claimed that Communists were behind the Supreme Court decision to outlaw school segregation. Senator James Eastland (Democrat, Mississippi), chairman of the Senate Internal Security Subcommittee, called the 1954 school desegregation decision an attempt "to graft into the organic law of the land the teachings, preachings and social doctrines [of] Karl Marx. . . . What other explanation could there be except that a majority of [the Supreme] Court is being influenced by some secret, but very powerful Communist or pro-Communist influence?" The Louisiana Joint Legislative Committee to Maintain Segregation, an official arm of the Louisiana legislature, brought in some professional ex-Communist witnesses willing to testify, falsely, that the National Association for the Advancement of Colored People was secretly Communist controlled.

The campaign to link civil rights to communism failed chiefly because it was untrue. While Communists had long championed the rights of black people and were among the most militant opponents of white racism in the 1920s and 1930s, the CPUSA played only a minor role in the civil rights movement of the 1950s and 1960s. The two chief civil rights organizations of the 1950s, the NAACP and the Urban League, had long kept their organization free of Communists. One major civil rights leader, A. Philip Randolph, head of the Brotherhood of Sleeping Car Porters, had worked with Communists in the late 1930s but soured on the relationship after the Nazi-Soviet pact; by the end of World War II he was a convinced anti-Communist. Randolph made sure that Communists and groups linked to the CPUSA were kept at arm's length from his greatest accomplishment, the 1963 civil rights March on Washington.

J. Edgar Hoover of the FBI regarded the civil rights movement with distaste and directed Bureau agents to follow up every hint of a Communist link, but they never found a significant Communist role. Hoover did determine that one of Martin

Luther King, Jr.'s advisers, the New York attorney Stanley Levinson, had once been part of the CPUSA's mechanism for laundering secret Soviet subsidies. Levinson, however, may have left the party in the late 1950s, and it was not clear that he was linked to the CPUSA after he became associated with King. Hoover took his information to Attorney General Robert Kennedy. Kennedy, in turn, informally told King of Levinson's background and urged him to break contact with him. King did not break with Levinson, but he did keep their relationship more circumspect. Hoover's discovery of Levinson's covert Communist background had other consequences, however. After Levinson's role was discovered, Hoover ordered the Bureau to tap King's phone and bug his meetings to discover if there was a serious Communist presence in King's inner circle. The taps and bugs showed that there was none beyond Levinson's role but revealed that in his private life King had a casual approach to sexual ethics. Hoover, who disliked King's civil rights agenda and was also of a puritanical disposition, leaked the information to the press in an unsuccessful attempt to discredit King's increasing stature as a national moral leader.

Just as in the antifascist era, there were episodes of popular violence against Communists, sometimes from the same groups that had once beaten up Nazi Bundists. In 1949 the Civil Rights Congress, a CPUSA front group, scheduled a fund-raising concert in Peekskill, New York. The proceeds of the concert were to assist the legal defense of the CPUSA leaders in the *Dennis* case. The concert's leading attraction was Paul Robeson, the highly talented black singer. Robeson was a longtime ally of the party, but what set off the local American Legion was a speech he gave shortly before the concert. According to reports, Robeson advised American blacks not to fight in a war against the Soviet Union. Hundreds of World War II veterans led by the Legion gathered at Peekskill on the day of the concert and blocked roads, rocked cars, harassed and threatened concertgoers, and forced cancellation of the event. When it was rescheduled, New York authorities sent in several hundred state police to prevent violence. Once again, furious war veterans assailed the concert site, but police protection was sufficient to allow the concert to proceed. The veterans, however, stoned the cars of those leaving the concert, and about 150 persons were injured. Police arrested Peekskill Legion officers for leading the violent protest, but a local grand jury refused to indict.

Communists charged, in the words of the writer Howard Fast, a leader of the Civil Rights Congress, that "the Peekskill affair was an important step in the preparation for the fascization of America and for the creation of receptive soil for the promulgation of World War III." It was not, and nothing illustrated that better than the decision of the Republican governor of New York to send in hundreds of state police to protect a Communist fundraising concert from angry American war veterans.

Beyond Peekskill there were similar, if less dramatic, physical assaults on Communist meetings at scattered sites around the nation, and instances of CPUSA organizers whose homes were vandalized. Particularly during the Korean War there were several dozen attacks on organizers for the few Communist-led unions that still existed. Some were badly beaten and physically thrown off work sites by enraged workers. The party and its various fronts also occasionally found it difficult to rent public or private meeting halls.

These instances of violence and of other causes seeking to use the banner of anticommunism illustrate the power of the issue. But the overlapping of the anti-Communist era with the civil rights era illustrates that anticommunism was only one, albeit a prominent one, of a multitude of concerns and issues that competed for public attention. Communism and anticommunism loomed large to a segment of the public, particularly to the politically engaged segment, but most Americans regarded communism, as they regarded all politics, as just one concern among many in life. In a 1949 public opinion poll on the most serious issue facing the nation, only 3 percent of the public placed communism first. More important issues included preventing war, inflation, government spending, taxes, relations with the Soviet Union, nuclear war, housing, and union-management turmoil.

Popular anti-Communist sentiment had not yet peaked in 1949, but the cold war was well under way, and *Amerasia*, Elizabeth Bentley, and the Hiss-Chambers affair had already appeared on the scene. Public concern about domestic communism reached a high point during the Korean War (1950–1953), and it became for several years one of the most highly charged political issues of the day, but the notion that most Americans were so obsessed with domestic Communists that hysteria ruled the land for more than a decade, a notion found in some historical accounts, is myth.

9

The End of the Anti-Communist Era

AFTER ITS PEAK during the Korean War, anticommunism remained pervasive, but the emotion and importance attached to the issue of domestic communism steadily subsided. Foremost among those factors reducing the intensity of anticommunism was Stalin's death in 1953. His Soviet successors never came close to matching him in ruthlessness or aggression, and his passing allowed international cold war tensions to ease. So too did the settlement of the Korean War along lines roughly reestablishing the status quo ante bellum. While America's nuclear monopoly could not be reestablished, by the mid-1950s the North Atlantic Treaty Organization (NATO) had stabilized the conventional military situation in Central Europe. In the late 1940s Red Army superiority in men and firepower in Europe was so massive that only American resort to nuclear war could have stopped a Soviet attack. By the mid-1950s American troop reinforcements, American financing of French and British military modernization, and the raising of an American-equipped West German army, all under a coordinated NATO military plan, had established a defensive force sufficient to have a reasonable chance against a Soviet conventional attack. The Marshall Plan also had given Western Europe the resources it needed to reestablish its economic and political health. In the late 1940s, amidst the turmoil and economic privation of the postwar period, the prospect of Communist parties coming to power in France, Italy, and Greece had been strong. By the mid-1950s this was a fading memory as Western Europe experienced a steady increase in its standard of living and social stability. In Eastern Europe violent popular revolts against Soviet rule in East Germany (1953) and Hungary (1956) and a near revolt in Poland (1956) also demonstrated the Soviets' uneasy hold over their empire. This was confirmed as well when Mao Tse-tung removed his regime from Moscow's tutelage in 1957–1958. The Sino-Soviet split left China under Communist rule, but it was no longer a Moscow satellite and ended the frightening image of a monolithic Moscow-led Red empire stretching from the Baltic to the South China Sea. All these international developments greatly diminished the apocalyptic overtones of the early years of the cold war.

The domestic partisan political element in the equation also changed. In 1952 Republicans won control of the presidency and both houses of Congress. With Eisenhower in control of the executive branch, Republicans assured the nation that the problem of Communist infiltration was over, that whatever laws were needed had been passed and were properly enforced, and that everything that needed to be done to combat domestic communism had been done. Democrats, who regarded the issue as a millstone around their neck, were happy to agree. The angriest section of conservative Republicans, those of the "old right," were unhappy with Eisenhower's moderate conservatism and wanted additional revenge inflicted on the Democrats. But they were a minority voice even within the Republican party. The Senate's censure of Joseph McCarthy and his subsequent ineffectiveness demonstrated the old right's isolation and declining importance. In 1956 the issue of domestic communism played only a minor role in the presidential election. By the 1960 presidential campaign, domestic communism was not an issue in dispute between the two parties.

Adding to the increasing public complacency toward domestic communism from the mid-1950s onward was the growing realization that the CPUSA was a broken movement. Looking back, it is clear that American communism's decisive defeat occurred in 1948–1950 when the Progressive party campaign failed and the

CPUSA lost its labor base with its expulsion from the CIO. With these two defeats it lost not only its bid to control American liberalism but its role as a significant force within the liberal and labor community. Most of the damage done to the Communist movement by the government's legal attacks and by congressional hearings occurred after it had lost the liberal civil war and after Philip Murray had decided to oust Communists from the CIO, a classic case of "beating a dead horse." Government attacks on domestic communism in the 1950s, however, further marginalized the CPUSA and prevented the reentry of Communists into the labor and liberal movements.

Even after the full weight of public and private hostility came down on the American Communist party in the early 1950s, the blow that nearly wiped out the party came from abroad, not from Joseph McCarthy or J. Edgar Hoover. Soviet leader Nikita Khrushchev's 1956 confirmation that Stalin had been a brutal monster so shattered Communist morale that the CPUSA lost three-quarters of its members in two years. By 1958 it could count only about three thousand members.

The American Communist party soldiered on, sustained by the faith of its hard core as well as by continued generous secret Soviet subsidies. Documents found in Soviet archives show that Soviet subsidies continued until the Soviet Union entered its terminal crisis, with secret payments in cash to Gus Hall, the CPUSA's general secretary, of $2 million in 1987 and $3 million in 1988. The Soviets cut off payments in 1989 after Hall criticized the efforts of Mikhail Gorbachev to reform the Soviet Union. The total of Soviet secret subsidies to the CPUSA in the 1980s was approximately $20 million.

All through the 1960s and 1970s the Communist party remained a pariah in American politics. By this time the FBI had established so many informants in the movement that it was unable to conduct the sort of semicovert political organizing that had served it so well in the 1930s and 1940s. And because of FBI penetration of the party, Soviet intelligence agencies no longer made use of its organization. Considering how battered and tiny the party was, by the 1960s and 1970s FBI resources devoted to the CPUSA were greatly disproportionate to the threat. The excessive nature of the FBI's infiltration and use of disruptive tactics against the CPUSA during this period, and similar treatment of the even smaller Trotskyist Socialist Workers party, was so great that it constituted unnecessary harassment. Trotskyists brought suit against the government over the extent of FBI coverage of their activities and won a substantial financial settlement from a sympathetic court. FBI surveillance relaxed in the late 1970s and 1980s, but even its reduced commitment occasionally scored a point. In 1989 Alan Thomson, executive director of the National Council of American-Soviet Friendship, one of the CPUSA's auxiliaries, was indicted for evading currency regulations by concealing a $17,000 Soviet cash subsidy that he had secretly brought back from the USSR. In June 1992 Thomson pled guilty. His plea agreement included the transcript of the FBI's concealed videotape of Thomson's handing over the $17,000, his discussion of the Soviet source of the funds, and his instructions on laundering the cash to a woman who turned out to be an FBI agent who had operated inside the Communist movement for years.

By the late 1950s the entire internal security apparatus that had been created in the late 1940s and early 1950s was disproportionate to the reduced threat posed by the Communist movement. It took some years for this imbalance to be understood. Much of the Communist party's success in the 1930s and 1940s had been achieved covertly as, for example, when it achieved a dominant role in CIO unions with 1,370,000 members, though only a handful of the hundreds of CIO Communist leaders ever admitted CPUSA membership. The secrecy that had once camouflaged success, in the 1950s hid failure. As time passed, of course, the reduced circumstances of the Communist party became clear to more and more people. Like many government programs, however, the internal security system kept working as if nothing had changed.

The reach of the internal security apparatus was gradually scaled back. As noted, Supreme Court decisions rendered the Smith Act and key sections of the McCarran Act useless by the late 1950s, and the Eisenhower administration never attempted to implement several sections of the latter. The Kennedy administration made a few efforts at reviving the Subversive Activities Control Board but eventually gave it up as a wasted effort. The agency had little to do during the 1960s, and in 1968 Congress removed most of its nominal functions. It was officially abolished in 1973.

Congressional committees continued to investigate domestic communism, but once the American Communist movement was clearly broken by the mid-1950s, public interest in congressional hearings sank like a stone and never recovered. By the 1960s HUAC and SISS were regarded as relics and had lost the power to intimidate or frighten. About the only time House Un-American Activities Committee hearings attracted major attention was when they were held in San Francisco or other cities where radical groups could muster large numbers of protesters and mount raucous demonstrations. HUAC attempted to gain a new lease on life with investigations of New Left radicalism in the late 1960s and early 1970s, but this went poorly. With its purpose established in a different era under a different context, HUAC was an awkward instrument for dealing with the amorphous New Left. Committee members kept looking for covert involvement by the CPUSA, but there was little. New Left radicalism contained many revolutionary extremists, including some engaged in violence. But the movement was disorganized, anarchistic, and without the CPUSA's covert ties to a foreign power. Nor did the New Left radicals who appeared as witnesses serve as useful foils for the committee. Communists had habitually looked and acted guilty by giving evasive testimony or taking the Fifth Amendment. Many of the New Left radicals who testified boasted of their revolutionary goals. American communism did contribute to the New Left, but only in an indirect way. A significant portion of the New Left's leaders and activists were "red-diaper babies," the sons and daughters of former Communists. They embraced their parents' radicalism but refused to enter the CPUSA with its history of ideological rigidity. As for the House Un-American Activities Committee, in 1969 its changed its name to the House Internal Security Committee. By this time a strong campaign against the committee had gained support among liberal Democrats, and it was abolished in 1975.

The broad anti-Communist consensus in American politics was not seriously questioned until the Vietnam War. In his 1961 inaugural address, President Kennedy had pledged to "pay any price, bear any burden, meet any hardship, support any friend, oppose any foe to assure the survival and the success of liberty." It was a sweeping commitment and one that was tested when the United States intervened in South Vietnam to suppress an insurrection backed by the Communist government in North Vietnam. Support for the war weakened as prospects for a quick military victory faded and South Vietnam was unable to develop a regime with sufficient mass support and internal dynamism to overcome Vietnam's Communists. Liberals particularly found it difficult to sustain their support for the war in the face of incessant pictures of American jets dropping napalm on the villages of Asian peasants.

In 1968 Senator Eugene McCarthy, who had entered politics twenty years earlier fighting Communists for control of Minnesota's Democratic-Farmer-Labor party, adopted an uncompromising antiwar position and challenged President Lyndon Johnson for the Democratic party's presidential nomination. McCarthy's campaign drove Johnson from the race, but Vice-President Hubert Humphrey, the quintessential anti-Communist liberal, won the presidential nomination. He then lost the election to Richard Nixon, the very embodiment of Republican anticommunism.

The McCarthy campaign in 1968 and the successful campaign of Senator George McGovern (Democrat, South Dakota) for the Democratic party's presidential nomination in 1972 destroyed the anti-Communist consensus that had prevailed in the Democratic party since 1948. After 1968 most prominent liberal leaders abandoned the type of anticommunism that had been dominant. Some simply shifted to a more restrained version, believing only that Kennedy had overstated the matter and that wars such as Vietnam were too high a price and too heavy a burden for too unworthy a friend. Others came to regard anticommunism as

inherently suspect. The most extreme wing of the antiwar movement openly championed the cause of the Vietnamese Communists. Many of the attitudes and beliefs of the Popular Front era
were revived, and even a few of the veterans of that era reentered mainstream politics. (McGovern himself had belonged
to the Progressive party.) This revival of Popular Front–like
attitudes, however, was not a revival of the Popular Front. The
Popular Front of the 1930s and 1940s had been a working political alliance between a segment of liberals and an American Communist party whose membership numbered more than fifty
thousand and which had significant institutional power in the labor
movement. The Communist party of the 1970s and 1980s remained tiny, perhaps fewer than five thousand members, and
worked only on the fringes of mainstream politics in a few scattered locations. The loose and uncoordinated New Left of the
anti–Vietnam War era had far more influence on the direction of
liberalism than did the orthodox Stalinists of the CPUSA.

    Although sentiments reminiscent of the Popular Front era—
hostility toward anticommunism and a benign view of communism—gained increasing sway over liberal activists and aca-
demics, Americans in general remained deeply anti-Communist.
Every political figure with national political ambitions felt it necessary to appear prepared to confront the Soviet Union. The national political consensus behind American cold war policies, a
commitment to NATO, and the maintenance of a large military
force capable of deterring the Soviet Union remained intact until
the cold war ended with the collapse of the USSR.

    During the 1970s and 1980s, American Communists also
faded from the public consciousness. Soviet communism and
other foreign communism remained a matter of public aware-
ness and concern, but not American communism. By the 1980s
the CPUSA was treated by the media as a quaint anachronism, the
subject of feature stories with the theme of "yes, there really is an
American Communist party" that had the same tone as a story
on the continued existence of the Shakers or some other nearly
forgotten antique from the American past.

There never was a single anti-Communist party or an anti-Communist ideology. Communism aroused the hostility of people on the right, the center, and the left. It was disliked by union leaders, by business executives, by Catholic priests and Protestant evangelists. American patriots disliked it as the ideology of America's chief foreign foe, East European ethnic Americans disliked it for what it had done to their former homelands, and liberal internationalists opposed it as a barrier to a world-wide democratic order. The only common thread of the different varieties of anticommunism was their disdain of communism. Thus an evaluation of anticommunism is inherently premised on an evaluation of communism.

The American Communist party was never large. It reached a peak membership of 65,000 to 70,000 just before and just after World War II, though its turnover was so rapid that perhaps half a million Americans were members at least briefly. In the short run the Communist party could mobilize an impressive number of activists for a given task because of the extraordinary number of cadre (several thousand at the party's height) who were employed full-time by the party or its auxiliaries and by the dedication of most party members. And there is no doubting that dedication. The party's longtime members were sincere, hard-working, and totally devoted to the movement.

From the mid-1930s to 1950 the CPUSA was a significant but never a major force in American society. In mainstream politics it was a consequential player in New York, California, Minnesota, Wisconsin, Michigan, Washington, and Oregon, and in 1948 it made a failed but ambitious bid to become a factor in national politics through Henry Wallace's Progressive party. Its greatest success was in the labor movement where it dominated the leadership of unions with a quarter of the CIO's membership. Its myriad front groups and auxiliary organizations gave it toeholds among immigrant groups, in the civil rights movement, on college campuses, and in Hollywood. One of the disturbing aspects of the party's activities during its heyday was its largely covert nature. Most Communists in the labor movement and in

mainstream politics hid their identity, and their activities were coordinated by clandestine Communist caucuses that were covertly
supervised by the CPUSA itself.

The American Communist party had been founded in emula-
tion of the Bolshevik revolution. Until Soviet communism itself
collapsed, the CPUSA accepted as definitive whatever interpretation of Marxism-Leninism prevailed in Moscow and always regarded the political, social, economic, and cultural arrangements
prevalent in the Soviet Union as the model for American society.
When Stalin ruled the Soviet Union, all American Communists
were Stalinists. During the height of Stalin's Great Terror in the
1930s, a purge that murdered millions, Stalin's rule received the
unqualified and unstinted endorsement of American Communists. When the American Communist party was at its greatest
strength, its goal was the destruction of American society and its
replacement by a state modeled on Stalin's Russia.

The American Communist party from its earliest years to the
end of Soviet communism was secretly financed by the Soviet
Union, and at every stage in its existence accepted and sought Soviet direction. While day-to-day management of the American
party was left to Americans, Soviet officials intervened at will on
matters great and small. Soviet orders were generally accepted
without argument. No American Communist leader ever successfully defied Moscow; those who tried were expelled. The
American Communist party's first loyalty was to the Soviet
Union, and it worked with and for Soviet intelligence agencies
engaged in espionage against the United States from the 1920s
onward. Three of the CPUSA's most influential general secretaries, Jay Lovestone (1927–1929), Earl Browder (1932–1945),
and Eugene Dennis (1945–1959), personally participated in Soviet espionage against the United States. The CPUSA created a secret apparatus that infiltrated and manipulated several U.S.
government agencies in the 1930s. The Communist underground also worked for Soviet intelligence, and a number of the
underground's participants became spies under direct Soviet
control. During World War II the American Communist party's
secret apparatus worked with and provided personnel who

assisted Soviet intelligence in stealing American atomic bomb secrets.

A movement as profoundly antidemocratic, as given to covert activity, and possessing the size and institutional resources of the CPUSA would have been a troubling presence in American society in any era. Although the movement was strongly attacked at its birth, for most of the 1920s and 1930s Americans actively opposed the Communist party but did not mobilize anti-Communist sentiment and made no serious attempt to destroy the party. After World War II the situation changed. The American Communist party became the internal ally of America's most dangerous foreign enemy, an enemy who was nuclear armed, expansionary, and ambitious for global hegemony. Before World War II the Communist party's activities had been troublesome, even occasionally scandalous, but tolerable; in the cold war era its activities were potentially dangerous and intolerable.

The cold war was not a war like World War II or even World War I, where military needs required the general mobilization of society. But neither was it peace. After 1948 the United States was in a state of low-level war mobilization, sustaining a military establishment and supporting a military industrial base many times the size of that previously maintained in times of real peace. Large numbers of American troops were stationed abroad and engaged in numerous cold war–related conflicts in which more than 100,000 died. Billions of dollars of American aid went abroad to support cold war allies. There was, in addition, the constant psychological pressure of maintaining a strategic nuclear capacity which, if ever used, would likely have been used in the context of a nuclear war with the Soviet Union that would have also destroyed most of the United States and ended modern civilization. This cold war mobilization required an anti-Communist consensus, a sort of negative ideological mobilization. This consensus could not be achieved in the presence of an American Communist party with the institutional power it possessed in the late 1940s.

The CPUSA was never outlawed, membership in the party was never a crime, and even during the height of the anti-Commu-

nist era it operated legally, maintained offices, published literature, recruited members, and sustained a network of auxiliary
organizations. It was, however, harassed, prosecuted, persecuted,
isolated, and reduced to an insignificant force. It is difficult
to imagine that the United States could have maintained its
forty-year commitment to the cold war had this not been accom-
plished. America's political system could not achieve the consensus needed for the cold war commitment while accommodating
within that system a political movement that adhered to the ideology and promoted the interests of the cold war enemy. For all
its sporadic ugliness, excesses, and silliness, the anticommunism
of the 1940s and 1950s was an understandable and rational response to a real danger to American democracy.

Selected Readings

DOMESTIC ANTICOMMUNISM: Earl Latham, *The Communist Controversy in Washington: From the New Deal to McCarthy* (Cambridge, Mass., 1966); Richard M. Fried, *Nightmare in Red: The McCarthy Era in Perspective* (New York, 1990); Richard Gid Powers, *Not Without Honor: The History of American Anticommunism* (New York, 1996); David Caute, *The Great Fear: The Anti-Communist Purge Under Truman and Eisenhower* (New York, 1978); John Earl Haynes, *Communism and Anti-Communism in the United States: An Annotated Guide to Historical Writings* (New York, 1987); Samuel Stouffer, *Communism, Conformity, and Civil Liberties: A Cross-Section of the Nation Speaks Its Mind* (Garden City, N.Y., 1955); Richard M. Freeland, *The Truman Doctrine and the Origins of McCarthyism: Foreign Policy, Domestic Politics, and Internal Security, 1946–1948* (New York, 1972); Robert W. Griffith and Athan Theoharis, eds., *The Specter: Original Essays on the Cold War and the Origins of McCarthyism* (New York, 1974); M. J. Heale, *American Anticommunism: Combating the Enemy Within, 1830–1970* (Baltimore, 1990); Ellen Schrecker, ed., *The Age of McCarthyism: A Brief History with Documents* (Boston, 1994).

DOMESTIC ANTIFASCISM: Leo P. Ribuffo, *The Old Christian Right: The Protestant Far Right from the Great Depression to the Cold War* (Philadelphia, 1983); David H. Bennett, *The Party of Fear: From Nativist Movements to the New Right in American History* (Chapel Hill, 1988); Geoffrey S. Smith, *To Save a Nation: American Countersubversives, the New Deal, and the Coming of World War II* (New York, 1973); Sander A. Diamond, *The Nazi Movement in the United States* (Ithaca, 1974); Leland V. Bell, *In Hitler's Shadow: The Anatomy of American Nazism* (Port Washington, N.Y., 1973); Morris Schonbach, *Native American Fascism During the 1930s and 1940s: A Study of Its Roots, Its Growth, and Its Decline* (New York, 1985).

CONGRESS AND ANTICOMMUNISM: Walter Goodman, *The Committee: The Extraordinary Career of the House Committee on Un-American Activities* (New York, 1968); August Raymond Ogden, *The Dies Committee: A Study of the Special House Committee for the Investigation of Un-American Activities, 1938–1944* (Washington, D.C., 1945); David M. Oshinsky, *A Conspiracy So Immense: The World of Joe McCarthy* (New York, 1983), and Thomas C. Reeves, *The Life and Times of Joe McCarthy* (New York, 1982); Eric Bentley, ed., *Thirty Years of Treason: Excerpts from Hearings Before the House Committee on Un-American Activities, 1938–1968* (New York, 1971); William A. Rusher, *Special Counsel: An Insider's Report on Senate Investigations into Communism* (New Rochelle, N.Y., 1968); Herbert L. Packer, *Ex-Communist Witnesses: Four Studies in Fact-Finding* (Stanford, 1962).

THE CHINA ISSUE: E. J. Kahn, Jr., *The China Hands: America's Foreign Service Officers and What Befell Them* (New York, 1975); Anthony Kubek, *How the Far East Was Lost: American Policy and the Creation of Communist China, 1941–1949* (Chicago, 1963); Paul G. Lauren, ed., *The China Hands: Legacy, Ethics and Diplomacy* (Boulder, Colo., 1987); Gary May, *China Scapegoat: The Diplomatic Ordeal of John Carter Vincent* (Washington, D.C., 1979); Steve W. Mosher, *China Misperceived: American Illusions and Chinese Reality* (New York, 1990); John N. Thomas, *Institute of Pacific Relations: Asian Scholars and American Politics* (Seattle, 1974); Robert P. Newman, *Owen Lattimore and the "Loss" of China* (Berkeley, 1992).

THE FBI AND ANTICOMMUNISM: Richard Gid Powers, *Secrecy and Power: The Life of J. Edgar Hoover* (New York, 1987); J. Edgar Hoover, *Masters of Deceit: The Story of Communism in America and How to Fight It* (New York, 1958); William Walton Keller, *The Liberals and J. Edgar Hoover: Rise and Fall of a Domestic Intelligence State* (Princeton, 1989); Kenneth O'Reilly, *Hoover and the Un-Americans: The FBI, HUAC, and the Red Menace* (Philadelphia, 1983); Athan G. Theoharis and John Stuart Cox, *The Boss: J. Edgar Hoover and the Great American Inquisition* (Philadelphia, 1988).

LIBERALS AND COMMUNISM: Alonzo Hamby, *Beyond the New Deal: Harry S. Truman and American Liberalism* (New York, 1973); Steven M. Gillon, *Politics and Vision: The ADA and American Liberalism, 1947–1985* (New York, 1987); Alan D. Harper, *The Politics of Loyalty:*

The White House and the Communist Issue, 1946–1952 (Westport, Conn., 1969); Mary Sperling McAuliffe, *Crisis on the Left: Cold War Politics and American Liberals, 1947–1954* (Amherst, Mass., 1978); Athan G. Theoharis, *Seeds of Repression: Harry S. Truman and the Origins of McCarthyism* (Chicago, 1971); John Earl Haynes, *Dubious Alliance: The Making of Minnesota's DFL Party* (Minneapolis, 1984); Norman D. Markowitz, *The Rise and Fall of the People's Century: Henry A. Wallace and American Liberalism, 1941–1948* (New York, 1973); Edward L. Schapsmeier and Frederick Schapsmeier, *Henry A. Wallace and the War Years, 1940–1965* (Ames, Iowa, 1970).

INTERNAL SECURITY: Harold Chase, *Security and Liberty: The Problem of Native Communists, 1947–1955* (Garden City, N.Y., 1955); Stanley I. Kutler, *The American Inquisition: Justice and Injustice in the Cold War* (New York, 1982); Peter L. Steinberg, *The Great "Red Menace": United States Prosecution of American Communists, 1947–1952* (Westport, Conn., 1984); Michael R. Belknap, *Cold War Political Justice: The Smith Act, the Communist Party, and American Civil Liberties* (Westport, Conn., 1977); Francis H. Thompson, *The Frustration of Politics: Truman, Congress, and the Loyalty Issue, 1945–1953* (Rutherford, N.J., 1979).

AMERICAN COMMUNISM: Harvey Klehr and John Earl Haynes, *The American Communist Movement: Storming Heaven Itself* (New York, 1992); Theodore Draper, *The Roots of American Communism* (New York, 1957) and *American Communism and Soviet Russia, the Formative Period* (New York, 1960); Harvey Klehr, *The Heyday of American Communism: The Depression Decade* (New York, 1984); Maurice Isserman, *Which Side Were You On? The American Communist Party During the Second World War* (Middletown, Conn., 1982); Joseph Starobin, *American Communism in Crisis, 1943–1957* (Cambridge, Mass., 1972); Guenter Lewy, *The Cause That Failed: Communism in American Political Life* (New York, 1990).

COMMUNISTS AND ESPIONAGE: Harvey Klehr, John Earl Haynes, and Fridrikh Igorevich Firsov, *The Secret World of American Communism* (New Haven, Conn., 1995); Herbert Romerstein and Stanislav Levchenko, *The KGB Against the "Main Enemy": How the Soviet Intelligence Service Operates Against the United States* (New York, 1989); Ronald Radosh and Joyce Milton, *The Rosenberg File: A Search for the Truth* (New York, 1983); Allen Weinstein, *Perjury: The Hiss-Chambers*

Case (New York, 1978); Whittaker Chambers, *Witness* (New York, 1952): Alger Hiss, *In the Court of Public Opinion* (New York, 1957); Elizabeth Bentley, *Out of Bondage* (New York, 1988); Harvey Klehr and Ronald Radosh, *The Amerasia Spy Case: Prelude to McCarthyism* (Chapel Hill, 1996); Robert Lamphere and Tom Shachtman, *The FBI-KGB War: A Special Agent's Story* (New York, 1986); Rebecca West, *The New Meaning of Treason* (New York, 1964)

COMMUNISM AND ANTICOMMUNISM IN THE LABOR MOVEMENT: Bert Cochran, *Labor and Communism: The Conflict That Shaped American Unions* (Princeton, 1977); Harvey A. Levenstein, *Communism, Anticommunism, and the CIO* (Westport, Conn., 1981); Max Kampelman, *The Communist Party vs. the C.I.O.: A Study in Power Politics* (New York, 1957); Roger Keeran, *The Communist Party and the Auto Workers Unions* (Bloomington, Ind., 1980).

COMMUNISM AND ANTICOMMUNISM IN CULTURE: Stephen J. Whitfield, *The Culture of the Cold War* (Baltimore, 1990); Daniel Aaron, *Writers on the Left: Episodes in American Literary Communism* (New York, 1959); Larry Ceplair and Steven Englund, *The Inquisition in Hollywood: Politics in the Film Community, 1930–1960* (Garden City, N.Y., 1980); Victor S. Navasky, *Naming Names* (New York, 1980); Robert Vaughn, *Only Victims: A Study of Show Business Blacklisting* (New York, 1972); Bernard F. Dick, *Radical Innocence: A Critical Study of the Hollywood Ten* (Lexington, Ky., 1988); Herbert Mitgang, *Dangerous Dossiers: Exposing the Secret War Against America's Greatest Authors* (New York, 1988).

Index

A NOTE ON THE AUTHOR

John Earl Haynes is a manuscript historian in twentieth-century American history at the Library of Congress. Born in Plant City, Florida, he studied at Florida State University, the University of California, Berkeley, and the University of Minnesota and has written widely on American communism and anticommunism. In addition to a great many articles, his books include *The Secret World of American Communism* (with Harvey Klehr and Fridrikh Igorevich Firsov), *The American Communist Movement* (with Harvey Klehr), and *Communism and Anti-Communism in the United States: An Annotated Guide to Historical Writings*.